Winning A

Winning At Work While Balancing Your Life

Career Coaching For Authentic Success

Dr. Scott Rosenthal
with Cynthia Peavler Bull

To order additional copies, please contact us.
BookSurge, LLC
www.booksurge.com
1-866-308-6235
orders@booksurge.com

Winning At Work While Balancing Your Life

TABLE OF CONTENTS

ACKNOWLEDGEMENTS

As our paths cross and we intersect daily with each other throughout the world, whether personally or secondarily via the news media or the Internet, we are touched by the common links we share as human beings.

We rejoice in triumphs and are saddened when life takes us down a path that contains a disappointing turn. However, we can find great strength in celebrating events that bring us hope and by storing up what we have gained for times when we need strength and hope. We can turn to each other for help and to God for guidance in all we encounter in life.

We believe that God has led us to write this book and to share it with you, our valued readers. Whether you are strong in your Christian beliefs or uncertain about your spiritual life, we trust this book brings you greater insight into approaching work and life issues from a Christian standpoint, and that it will encourage you on your faith journey.

Throughout our lives there have been many powerful influences that lend their presence to this writing—loved ones and clients, associates and strangers. But none is greater than God and our continuing relationship with Him.

I, Dr. Scott Rosenthal, extend many thanks to Doug Sherman for his longstanding inspiration, and to my wife for her patience and the rest of my family for their love and support.

I, Cynthia Peavler Bull, could not have been more pleased when Dr. Rosenthal asked me to join him in this endeavor. My sincere appreciation also goes to my loving husband for his support.

With heartfelt appreciation, we seek to provide you with

information to help you win battles in your daily living, and we invite you to share your lives with us. Please accept our invitation to assist you in any way by contacting us at Scott@CareerImpact. org or info@cynrje.com.

Sincerely,

Dr. Scott Rosenthal

Cynthia Peavler Bull

THE AUTHORS

D r. Scott Rosenthal, President of Career Impact and Co-Director of CrossRoads Group, offers career and life coaching to enhance your personal and professional life. A Program Developer, he has coached thousands of individuals in the areas of personal and professional development, including setting life goals and plans. He is a doctoral level, state licensed counselor who studied under Dr. Larry Crabb, best-selling author of numerous books, including *Connecting*. Dr. Rosenthal is the co-founder of the two successful consulting and coaching firms mentioned above with hundreds of organizational and individual clients. In addition, he is an ordained minister who successfully started a new church. His most recent published work, *Maximizing Your Leadership Potential—From God's Perspective*, can be found at his website along with other publications recommended by Career Impact. To learn more about Dr. Rosenthal, his organizations and his career and life coaching programs, visit www.careerimpact.org.

Cynthia Peavler Bull has successfully parlayed 35+ years as an independent businessperson and a 27-year counseling career into her passion—writing. She writes and edits for clients internationally on topics that include self-development, spirituality and personal experience, medicine, business and marketing. In 1967, she received a B. S. degree in Psychology and has worked in psychiatric hospitals and community mental health agencies in Virginia and Ohio. Concurrently, she owned five successful businesses operating consecutively for 18 years during her 35-year entrepreneurial career. Cynthia earned a Diploma in Medical Language and Transcription Studies from

At-Home Professions in 1997. Currently she provides writing, editing and transcription services on a freelance basis. She is the author of *How To Be A Medical Transcriptionist: A Beginner's Guide To Real Facts And Inside Secrets That Lead To A Successful Career*. Cynthia is also a published poet appearing in *America At The Millennium: The Best Poems And Poets of the 20TH Century*. Visit her at www.cynrje.com for more information or to contract with her.

PREFACE

A Roadmap to Sanity

"For the Word of the God is living and active. Sharper than any double-edged sword, it penetrates even to dividing soul and spirit, joints and marrow; it judges the thoughts and attitudes of the heart. Nothing in all creation is hidden from God's sight. Everything is uncovered and laid bare before the eyes of Him to whom we must give account." Hebrews 4:12-13

After an especially harrowing morning, I stopped at the post office to pick up mail and asked postmistress Penny, "Do you have anywhere in here a roadmap to sanity?"

With an understanding smile she replied, "No, but I'll keep looking."

After talk about the war, her 20-year-old son's upcoming deployment to Iraq and her faith in prayer for his safekeeping, I proceeded to the bank to make a deposit. Donna was already at the drive-up window ready for a customer.

I shared with her my conversation with Penny and asked if the bank had a roadmap to sanity. After replying, "No, not here!" and then a reflective pause, as though looking deep within her soul, she said, "You know, every morning for an hour I go for a walk alone, with my dog, where there's no music, no TV, and have time to think. You know, I just...Well, I just talk to God. That's the only time I really have peace."

"I understand completely," I replied. "The world is just getting way out of control, at least in our society."

"Yes. I think about how I'm an employee, a wife, I have my interests and all these things to do...but then there's all this other stuff." As she stood with a sincere, soulful, though somewhat perplexed look on her face, I continued.

"I know what you mean. And there's always someone very willing to give you *their* stuff—without asking *your* permission! AND, they expect you to either do it or solve their problem in some way, without taking any responsibility for it!"

To which Donna exclaimed, "Yeah!"

Driving home, it occurred to me that God had once again given me an answer; that one of the solutions to finding a pathway to peace in life was found in the conversations I had just had with Penny and Donna.

The problem is that we've lost our relationship with God. The solution to finding the pathway to peace, a roadmap to sanity, is the same: a close relationship with God.

Sure, we may have time set aside for God, church and our religious routines, but they may have little to do with actual faith and spending time with God. If we call ourselves Christians but aren't sure who our boss is, how can we possibly reap the benefits of all He has prepared for us? In the midst of all the confusion that invades and permeates our lives, how can we learn to recognize His voice and listen for His Word? How can we know of His greatness?

Yes, God does speak to us, but often we are too busy to listen. And when we stop listening for God's voice or watching for His messages, we tend to misplace Him, like so many other "things" in our lives. Our roadmap to sanity is found in God's Word.

INTRODUCTION

Who Is Your "Real" Boss?

"Whatever you do, work at it with all your heart, as working for the Lord, not for men, since you know that you will receive an inheritance from the Lord as a reward. It is the Lord Christ you are serving."
Colossians: 3:23-24

Many of us feel trapped these days, whether on or off the job, and sometimes it's hard to define why we feel this way. It doesn't really matter what the circumstances are that caused the feelings or that got us to this point. The result is that we feel something has control over us, that we no longer guide our own destiny, and that the path we travel becomes darkened by negative circumstances that seem to surround us. Our field of mental and emotional vision narrows and we're left with the impression that "someone" else controls our master switch.

Let's not forget that as spiritual beings we suffer at spiritual levels as well, potentially leaving even deeper scars. What's also upsetting is the haze that clouds our thinking and keeps us feeling confused. Confusion and scars about what? About life in general.

In today's culture it is so easy to get caught up in whatever the world is trying to sell us through the media or in the marketplace, and this frenzy adds pressure to our already hectic pace. Competition encourages thoughts of "Me first," "If it's to be, it's up to me," "Look out for #1," and "Pulling your own strings." Part of what we sense is that we've been sold a "bill of goods." It seems we're always being told to "hurry," "rush," "do it now" in almost any situation we find ourselves, whether at home or on the job. We're made to feel that we must "take on more" and that what we do, no matter how well we do it, is never enough. All of this puts a tremendous strain on our lives, often without our full awareness.

Our bookstores are replete with best-selling self-help, humanistic based psychological theories filled with bold promises of thinking positively about "who is important around here." True, there are many voices we should listen to—government leaders, family members, good friends, wise counsel and the like—but in the midst of these clamoring messages, is there any way to find out what is really true? Who should I really be looking out for? Why am I here in the first place? What are the results of my efforts?

The problem is that we have stopped living our lives based on enduring principles and values that give us life and light to move through each day. Many of us have forgotten how to think, how to process our thoughts with our feelings, and vice versa. Why? Because there is no time allotted for such matters. Further, we have become desensitized to time alone, to spending time with God and reflective time alone.

What's worse is that "time" often seems to have overtaken us to the point that there *is* no time. We end up resenting that reality and feel cheated. If we're lucky enough to have a job, this resentment is compounded by jobs that take so much of our weekly time. Extended travel to and from work and traffic jams have become a regular part of the workweek for many.

How did we ever allow this lack of control to happen and *what* exactly has happened? Most of us work in jobs we don't particularly like for people we don't particularly respect. Somehow, we have become caught in a maze of uncertainty, and it affects us mentally, emotionally, and spiritually.

Why do we become so unhappy with, angry at and frustrated by our jobs? When we begin employment, most of us are eager, motivated and content. We initially feel challenged and energetic, but frequently with time we become depressed. Exactly when did we start resenting our boss and having an attitude of defiance?

But let's cut to the chase. In the marketplace who is in charge? Why, it's "the boss." It could be an immediate supervisor, or your ultimate boss might be your customers, stockholders or stakeholders. Or you may report directly to the CEO / President.

The truth is you have more than one boss and there are many fine, intelligent and well-meaning people in some type of authoritative position over you, if not all the time, then perhaps during certain projects, seasons of time, or periods. Taking this notion to the extreme, almost anyone could become your boss without you even realizing it, let alone those easily recognized by the stripes on their sleeves or their name on the company organizational chart.

And this, friends, is precisely the point. Until we stop, decide and declare who *really* is the ultimate boss in our lives, we will be killing time like a squirrel in his circular cage. Around and around he goes with nowhere to go. Feeding time is the long-awaited prize for this endless monotony, broken up only by a morsel of cheese now and then.

You see, whether we realize it or not, our "Boss" is God Himself. In the Bible's New Testament, the author is writing to the predominant group of workers of the day (similar to customer service personnel or salesclerks of today) who are struggling with these same issues.

While we agree that we are to respect and honor many of the voices that clamor for our attention and direct our lives, ultimately there is only "one boss" we must follow and obey. That "Boss" is God, our Lord Jesus Christ.

The theme of this book is concerned with surviving and thriving in the workplace, such that we can enjoy a healthy professional, personal and family life. Our book examines questions and issues Christians pose about how to live on a day-in and day-out basis in a tough, secular work world where sometimes you may be asked either to take a wrong course or actually ordered to do so.

Further, because there is so much collective garbage stored in our heads from lies we believe or half-truths we hold as convictions, we urge you to begin a journey (if you haven't already) of taking out the trash. We want to replace errors in your thinking and any cobwebs you have accumulated with fresh, pure wisdom from the Word of God, His Holy Bible.

In our book we present actual work problems that have troubled our clients over the years. However, as we share their stories with you, you will uncover wonderful opportunities that God presents through the disguise of problems, heartaches, disappointments and even tragedies. Contained in these accounts are practical solutions to real life situations.

As you continue reading, be prepared for a mindset adjustment that may occur and for the resulting benefits. It is the express design of this book to share biblical principles that open new avenues to help you solve problems and resolve differences. Although our setting is the workplace, the principles you read about can be applied to everyday life experiences, and we'll leave it to your own creativity to look within your life for solutions beyond your current situation. We make a distinction between God as your "Boss" and having a physical boss, because herein lies the issue of faith.

Obeying Your "Real" Boss

"Your Word is a lamp to my feet and a light for my path." Psalm 119:105

From the scriptures we learn that God is our real boss and that He has given us His Word and His Holy Spirit to guide us. This wisdom can help us sift through all that comes at us each day. Some days it seems like we are asked to do more than there is actually time for, but that's not God. God will give you the time to do all that He asks of you.

The million-dollar question of "Who is asking you?" is followed by the bonus question of "Why do we feel we must do it today or now?" If Christ is our real boss, that sort of changes our priorities, doesn't it? It changes who and what we listen to. It changes how we spend our time and what we think or worry about. The good news is that He is a good boss who wants to give you, and all of us, a fresh start.

> "Because of the Lord's great love we are not consumed, for His compassions never fail. They are new every morning; great is your faithfulness. I say to myself, 'The Lord is my portion; therefore I will wait for Him.' The Lord is good to those whose hope is in Him, to the one who seeks Him." Lamentations 3:22-25

That can be a very comforting verse. But for some reading this, it's a bit harder to grasp the truth and love spoken about.

Probably everyone who has ever worked has been through trials in the workplace at one time or another, some of which have left deeper scars than others. Some struggles have resulted in pain, difficulty and disappointment. For example, you have been let down by trusting others, or perhaps you have even resolved a time or two in exasperation, having been angered by coworkers or a boss: "If anything is going to happen around here, it's going to happen because of me (maybe even for me?)."

From our collective 50 years of counseling Christians in the marketplace, you will discover top issues Christians struggle with the most as they live with the reality of a heavenly boss juxtaposed amid the cadence of earthly "masters" or "authority voices" (even our own at times), a collection of frustrations, questions and problems heard most often. From their situations you will see that you are not alone.

We trust you will find wisdom and practical advice in the pages to come. Perhaps God is having you read this book because He wants to use you to share with those in need when the time comes. One of our goals is to help you prepare.

Questions and Issues

"But the fruit of the Spirit is love, joy, peace, patience, kindness, goodness, faithfulness, gentleness and self-control. Against such things there is no law." Galatians 5:22-23

O ur main treatise in the sections that follow is that biblical principles found in the scriptures are also solutions to many of our daily plights. Like a life raft to a drowning man, these precepts have literally saved the lives of millions of people just like you in one way or another. In accepting that God is our real boss, we have humbly sought His instruction, encouragement and enlightenment as we have taken to Him our clients' pressing issues, questions and problems, knowing full well that it is completely within His power to give them—and you, yes, each reader viewing these pages—even more light and wisdom through His Holy Spirit than they ever thought possible. Join us as we walk through "downtown anywhere" to see what keeps people awake at night, interrupts their peace, but also offers strength.

In **Part I**, you will discover how to face obstacles and deal with seemingly unsolvable problems and how the "fruit of the Spirit" bring guidance, healing, endurance, peace and even joy to difficult situations. Specifically, you will read about the following questions that we have separated into three categories of related concerns.

Primary Work Related Concerns
- Where is job security with layoffs and downsizing?

- What do you do with a boss you don't like?
- What do you do when you are required to put in more hours than you'd like?
- As a salesperson, how can I sell well against competition and still "love my neighbor"?
- Every time I try and share my faith, I get stepped on.
- What do you do when you dislike your coworkers or are dissatisfied in your job?
- How do you know when it's time to move on?
- How do I discover God's will for business decisions and my career?
- How can I incorporate prayer in the middle of the day? I know I need God's help on phone calls, with meetings and projects.
- If Jesus Christ is my real boss, how come I don't sense His presence and power?
- I see this huge gap between my faith on Sunday morning and the "real world" Monday through Sunday. I don't want to make work a "Sunday School" class, but still I need some practical tips to make my faith stronger throughout each day.

Secondary Home and Family Concerns

- How can I balance work and family life?
- My job has become a wedge between my spouse and me. It's the enemy.
- How do you build any kind of marital relationship when both spouses work outside the home (which is 90% of the cases)?

General Life Concerns

- I experience tremendous stress each day. How can my faith practically help me here?
- What kind of spiritual warfare am I likely to encounter in a secular marketplace and how should I handle it?
- How do I cope with failure, setbacks and trials?

Part II focuses on these examples of **Career Counseling Issues**.

- A recently divorced parent sleeping in a one-room apartment with three kids needs to take a job at McDonald's to show responsibility for child support.
- A laid-off executive is so fearful of lack of employment that he makes 70 networking visits in his first 7 weeks. (This is more than most clients will do in 6 months.)
- A gentleman has no support from his spouse. She comments upon seeing him at the computer, "At least you're doing something productive now."
- Countless wives have given their husbands the ultimatum, "Either you find a job by X day or I'm leaving." (How's that for 'til death do us part?)
- Type "A" businesswoman wants to leave her home and family because she is not moving fast enough up the corporate ladder. She feels she needs $150,000.
- A businesswoman was lied to upon hiring at a local bank. Rather than speak poorly about management, she takes the high road and walks with integrity.
- A successful entrepreneur (around 50 years old) decides to sell his business so he can have more time for ministry and community development interests. He now leads a tremendous outreach to the inner city.
- Many clients sit at home and wait for the phone to ring. They are too afraid to call someone they don't know and lack faith that God is moving in and through their process.
- A young college graduate from Africa refuses to join all of his peers. His fellow countrymen went ahead and got jobs without the proper paperwork, which is illegal. The young graduate waited until he was legal and is now suffering the temporary consequences of a tight job market.

I, Dr. Scott Rosenthal, extend many thanks to Doug Sherman for his longstanding inspiration, and to my wife for her patience and the rest of my family for their love and support.

I, Cynthia Peavler Bull, could not have been more pleased when Dr. Rosenthal asked me to join him in this endeavor. My sincere appreciation also goes to my loving husband for his support.

PART I

Primary Work Related Concerns

Where is job security with layoffs and downsizing?

"It is better to take refuge in the LORD than to trust in man." Psalm 118:8

According to a recent *USA Today* statistic, 75% of American workers are dissatisfied on the job. One expects global and domestic governmental and economic changes to impact our work history here in the United States, as demonstrated by economists' and sociologists' forecasts and data. The work ethic of recent generations (within 100 years) has changed significantly due to technical advances and more recently due to internal factors such as corporate scandals, which have affected millions of workers and contributed to increased layoffs and downsizing.

Our concern is with practical implications these changes have put on the workforce, as well as the work spirit as a whole, by bringing about pressures to both employer and employee. Particularly over the past decade, corporate "dis-reputation" has brought about devastating and life-altering situations for many workers, hitting every strata of the work continuum.

So, where does one find job security? It's important to remember just *who* is the boss. Christian principles teach that man cannot serve God and man. If we recall the problem and the solution as being one equation, we remind ourselves to make God our focus: God is the solution to the problem.

The reality is that our trust in "job security" is misplaced if it is placed in any job. Whoever our "boss" may be, that person is not our *real* boss, because no one takes the place of God in our lives: not at home, not at work, not in our activities, philanthropic or otherwise. We work for Him, and once we realize that God gave us the job in the first place, then, although we may have lost it by whatever reason, it is God who will present another job opportunity for us in His timing. It is He who determines when, where and how the opportunity will come. He provides us with resources from the past and the present for the future. He is constantly building resources within us to do His work.

If, in your daily routine, you've strayed from thinking of God as your boss, remind yourself to think of Him as your ultimate boss. No matter what man has offered you, it cannot compare to what God's plan is for your life. If you've looked to others to provide you with job security, remember that God is the *source* of security in all areas of your life. Visit with Him and discuss your concerns.

How can you get back in touch with God if you've "been away" or "gotten out of communications with Him"?

Although the answer may seem to be a complicated one because of "life" circumstances, it boils down to this: Look deep within to when God first made Himself known to you. You may have been a young child, or maybe at some point in your life you felt a glimpse of Him in your spirit but never pursued His calling. Or maybe you don't feel "worthy" of His time and attention because of the way you have lived your life to this point.

The fact is He is holding an appointment open and waiting to talk with you about anything.

"But," you ask, "what if He doesn't talk? What happens then?"

He will listen while you talk, either with words or in silent prayer. God hears our hearts, not just our words. The key to finding Him is found in that quiet voice or that small memory He planted deep within your spirit years earlier, perhaps when you were a small child. And for that you must search your soul to the origin of His Presence, to that place where He first invited you to enter into His Grace. Even though you may have forgotten God, He never forgets you.

With God as your boss, you need not fear layoffs or downsizing or working in a situation that brings about stress and disruption in your life. His purpose is for you to fulfill His plan in the job you have now and in any job you will have in the future. Keep Him uppermost in your focus as you face each day's tasks, as you run the gamut of trials and errors, and be secure in the knowledge that you will succeed according to His purpose.

Exercise #1

Questions for Small Group Discussion and / or Personal Reflection

1. Where do you turn to find a sense of job security?

2. 75% of American workers report being dissatisfied in their work. Why do you think this is?

3. What advice would you give a Christian friend who shares with you about his / her lack of fulfillment on the job?

Activities

Go to the Lord in prayer. Ask Him to reveal to you other sources you may have trusted for security and fulfillment apart from Him.

List the qualities and type of work environment that would actually help you feel more fulfilled and satisfied. To what extent can you work to implement these characteristics? Take one step.

What do you do with a boss you don't like?

"If it is possible, as far as it depends on you, live at peace with everyone." Romans 12:18

Unless you own your own business, you have a "physical" boss when you are employed. When you work for someone else, you are most generally hired to provide a product or a service, or to facilitate that product or service in some way. Whether you work on an assembly line, create pastries, are a sports figure, work in an office or build cars, somewhere there is a boss to whom you report. If you hold a position in management and your job is to oversee the work of others, you are held accountable to a boss and perhaps to a board or committee as well. Even when working as an independent contractor, your client becomes your boss, because you are providing a product or service for him or her until a project is completed.

No one enjoys having to answer to a boss who is unpleasant, or one who irritates or berates you or your coworkers, or one who simply is annoying in attitude, behavior or mannerisms. Remembering always that God is your *real* boss makes unpleasant situations tolerable and endurance possible, and He expects you to rely on His Word for guidance when problems arise.

"Peter and the other apostles replied: 'We must obey God rather than men!'" Acts 5:29

Due to federal and state guidelines governing work policy,

recourses are in place to protect employees as well as employers in the case of extreme disagreement. In theory, it is possible for an unhappy employee to seek recourse against perceived or actual unfair actions by an employer or by another employee. Recourse procedures exist in government facilities and in most businesses, certainly in corporations and most small businesses. They are designed to address and resolve conflicts with equitable results. In reality, sometimes these systems work and sometimes they don't.

You must remember that personality clashes are different from actual infractions against you. The latter are generally fairly well defined, and you will want, and need, to keep records of any that occur which might lead you to seek recourse action. Many people find themselves in situations where personality differences form the basis for dislike of superiors and contribute to an employee's disgruntled attitude. Add gossip and the "misery loves company" element, and the stage is set for job discontentment. Here we get into the realm of personal discipline, self-control, and looking inwardly to find our real meaning and purpose for being on the job. Again, we come back to where we place our focus. Is it on man...or God?

Frequently, the "personality" of a boss is defined based on job description rather than true personal identity, and a boss may defer to his or her work persona rather than allow the personality to come forth. A company must maintain order and someone must be in charge. If you don't like your boss because of personality differences, you may need to examine which personality it is that's causing the problem. Being able to separate the person from the job might make a difference in how well you can work with them.

People in today's workplace may tend to be more cautious about job security as a whole, and almost everyone experiences stress to some degree regardless of office or company size. By putting the shoe on the other foot and stepping outside one's personal frame of reference to consider what a fellow coworker might be experiencing, whether peer or boss; to offer a supportive word rather than a criticism; such efforts on your part may mean the difference between keeping your job and getting laid off or fired, and a difference in the amount of stress you experience.

Stress is a powerful and deceptive force that we tend to perceive as being caused from something or someone outside ourselves, but we experience it internally. Stress represents a struggle between external triggers that ignite internal memories, resulting in confused thoughts and perplexed emotions. It's easy to point to the boss as the problem. Without real cause to do so, however, it is frequently our inner conflicts poised in the work setting that produce stress, and it is human nature to blame others.

If you can remove actual causes for conflict, then you need to look deeper within yourself to find a cause for disliking your boss and to avoid placing your boss in the role of scapegoat. You may find that the real conflict is not with your boss but with yourself and perceived missed opportunities or disappointments. Remembering **Romans 12:18**, we need to try harder to "live at peace." Liking your coworkers or boss is a benefit and a privilege.

Exercise #2

Questions for Small Group Discussion and / or Personal Reflection

1. What is your relationship like with your boss at work?

2. Describe how you would like it to be.

3. What can you do to enhance your relationship with your boss?

4. As you think about God as your real "Boss," what questions, ideas, comments, concerns and observations do you have?

5. How would you like to honor God as your real boss?

Activities: "Work out" Project Options

If Jesus were to meet you at your place of work on Monday

morning, what would you want to discuss with Him about your vocation? Transform this question into a prayer and offer it to God.

Mark one day next week on your calendar to schedule reminders throughout the day to offer God thanksgiving, ask for help, etc.

What do you do when you are required to put in more hours than you'd like?

"May the God who gives endurance and encouragement give you a spirit of unity among yourselves as you follow Christ Jesus, so that with one heart and mouth you may glorify the God and Father of our Lord Jesus Christ." Romans 15:5-6

There are several options here, each having possible consequences:

1. Do the work but lose time with family or miss out on other plans.
2. Refuse to do the work but risk reprimand or firing.
3. Trade with someone to cover for the work but miss extra pay.

There is another, less negative option: Accept that this is part of the job and perform it to the best of your ability. Your attitude is all-important here and the answer lies in your perspective about the choices you have.

While we can never know what God's complete plan is for our lives, He does allow opportunities for us to test our willingness to be obedient—to Him and to others. During a job interview it is our responsibility to inquire about any extra or unexpected job demands that might arise. If occasional extra work or overtime is required and we are informed about it, then we will be prepared. However, there may be a fine line between doing what occasionally exceeds the norm and performing excessive or repeated patterns. If this happens and you feel that you are experiencing undue consequences, make your concerns known to your supervisor. Remember, you can always re-examine your career options.

Those extremes aside, God tells us that we are to have patience. He also tells us that we should have zeal in our efforts, that our willingness to go beyond what is expected of us reflects our obedience to Him as well as to our earthly boss, to whom we are to give our allegiance and support.

"Because of the service by which you have proved yourselves, men will praise God for the obedience that accompanies your confession of the gospel of Christ, and for your generosity in sharing with them and with everyone else." 2 Corinthians 9:13

Occasional extra work can be expected to occur in any job and may come at inconvenient times, but generally we survive and reschedule events without much difficulty. Remember, you can always take a step back and take some time to re-examine your career options. Keep in mind that God gave you the job you have and is in charge of your career transition. He has given you talents and abilities to use, abuse or lose. The choice is yours and He is very interested in the job decisions you make.

Exercise #3

Questions for Small Group Discussion and / or Personal Reflection

1. Which time management option for dealing with "work requirement overload" is the best one for you, given your specific circumstances?

2. Of all your work requirements, which ones need to be kept but rescheduled?

3. How can you adjust your calendar to accommodate these tasks?

Activities

Create or modify your job description to more accurately describe your current responsibilities. (Most job descriptions are either outdated or don't really exist in written form.)

Discuss your job requirements with your boss. In this meeting you can address significant issues such as competing time demands and role expectations.

Pray about your job requirements. Are there any that require an attitude change? Are there any that need to be addressed right now? What steps need to be taken to both honor God in your job and make it more realistically accomplishable?

As a salesperson, how can I sell well against competition and still "love my neighbor"?

"Similarly, encourage the young men to be self-controlled. In everything set them an example by doing what is good. In your teaching show integrity, seriousness and soundness of speech that cannot be condemned, so that those who oppose you may be ashamed because they have nothing bad to say about us." Titus 2:6-8

This question deals with honor and integrity. It is possible to compete with someone and still respect the differences that distinguish them from you. A salesperson is selling more than just a product or service. To a significant degree, the salesperson also sells himself or herself to a prospective client. This is a natural process of the promotional component, because the more the seller believes in the product or service, the more likely the client is to buy.

The tendency is to view the sales situation and the people in it from a global perspective rather than in a more linear view, needing to incorporate all of who the seller is and what they represent into what they promote.

Competition is an accepted element of marketing, the idea that somehow I must best my competitor to win the prize—the sale. But the competition factor tends to be blown out of proportion, separating "us" from "them" and causing disharmony between the parties involved. This is true whether competitors work for the same or different companies. If left unchecked, the situation can become a battle of us versus them.

Inherent are implied elements of secrecy, possible deception, and mistrust.

Competition is encouraged in most businesses, and when used in a healthy atmosphere, it motivates employees to reach company as well as personal standards of excellence. But when shady practices are used to encourage competition, this burden can weigh heavily on ethical sellers and carry negative consequences.

But this is a secular view, not a Godly one. In honest competitions we strive to do our best regardless of who our competitors are, motivated significantly by an internal drive to excel. The idea that I can't "love my neighbor" stems from insecurity, doubt and fear, and it is planted by the world to keep us separate, one from another.

God intends for us to do our best in all things in order that we may fulfill His plan for our lives. If we have a job that places us in competition with others, our focus should be on the outcome by His design. If you approach your task, your salesmanship, with honesty and integrity in your heart and respect for your competitors, then your focus, by His design, brings about goodness.

God wants us to do our best at all times and in all situations. When internal signals ignite against our "competitors" telling us to somehow beware of the "unknown," talk with God about how to approach your circumstances. He has the answer and we should always rely on God's Word to show us the way in any situation.

> "Do not seek revenge or bear a grudge against one of your people, but love your neighbor as yourself. I am the LORD." Leviticus 19:18

Exercise #4

Questions for Small Group Discussion and / or Personal Reflection

1. Whether you are actually in the sales profession or not, with whom do you tend to compete the most (at work, socially, athletically, etc.)?

2. What is a biblical response to competition you could see adapting?

Activities

1. Let someone pass you the next time you are on the freeway. What feeling does that conjure up inside of you?

2. What qualities in general distinguish a Christian competitor in work, sports or life? Share an example of someone you can look up to in this regard.

Every time I try and share my faith, I get stepped on.

"Be strong and courageous. Do not be afraid or terrified because of them, for the LORD your God goes with you; He will never leave you nor forsake you." Deuteronomy 31:6

onsider this question: Are you a soapbox or a gentle breeze? When you talk to coworkers or anyone about your faith, your delivery is everything. Their receptiveness to your message greatly depends on the manner in which you tell people about God, your faith, your beliefs. In today's society as a whole, speaking of God and one's faith carries risks. The dangers of evil and destruction lurk in our schools, our courts, our places of business. No longer are we guaranteed safety from violent eruptions of behavior despite our attempts to protect ourselves. Almost daily our newspapers and the evening news resound with acts of violence outside those inherent in war. Christians expect non-Christians to be uncomfortable hearing about God, but even some Christians are uncomfortable sharing their faith in an atmosphere of potential turbulence. But we are to have courage.

God wants us to share His good news and He wants us to do it with enthusiasm and joy in our hearts. We are to look to Him for guidance in all things. We are to seek wisdom to guide us, so that when we speak to others of our faith, the peace we carry in our hearts will naturally convey to them. Through our words and actions, our demeanor, we represent the invitation of salvation that God reserves for each of us.

"Whoever gives heed to instruction prospers, and blessed is he who trusts in the LORD. The wise in heart are called discerning, and pleasant words promote instruction. Understanding is a fountain of life to those who have it, but folly brings punishment to fools. A wise man's heart guides his mouth, and his lips promote instruction." Proverbs 16:20-23

To choose your words carefully and wisely takes conscious effort and awareness. It requires that you speak with God about what He wishes you to share with others and the manner in which you are to share it. The focus is on Him, not our inadequacies, which He strengthens.

We should always be ready to share God's Word, and when we listen closely for and to Him, He places us at the right moment in someone's life to give comfort, support, encouragement, joy, or to simply be silent and present with them. There are also times we know most certainly that He has placed us where He specifically needs us to be. So you must ask yourself, "Does God want me to randomly share His message, or does He have a special purpose and time for His message?"

One of the best ways to help someone understand how to become a Christian is to use one of the excellent booklets like "The Four Spiritual Laws" or "The Bridge." These illustrate and explain God's story extremely well, having been used for decades to help people share their faith in Christ.* One can usually find such booklets in the back of a church lobby (in a brochure rack of some type), or in a Christian bookstore.

If you experience doubt about sharing God's Word, maybe it's time to have a personal talk with Him. There will always be those who are uncomfortable hearing His Word. But when He really needs to speak to someone, He gives the messenger the right words spoken in the tone that the listener who needs to hear Him will recognize. When you feel hesitation, look to God for strength to deliver His message with confidence.

*Sometimes the best way to share your faith in Christ is to purpose to develop a relationship with the person God may be calling you to reach. Once you get to know one another, the topic is usually much better received than "cold" attempts of "persuasion."

Exercise #5

Questions for Small Group Discussion and / or Personal Reflection

1.   How might God want you to share His message? Who would you speak with first?

2.   In your own words, jot down some ideas below as to what you might say to convey His message.

Activities: "Work out" Project Options

1.   In prayer, ask God to reveal someone at work who needs prayer. Document below the person's name and area of need. Pray for that individual now.

2.   What is it about the evangelism process that makes you the most uncomfortable? Visualize yourself confident, articulate and at peace during an instance where you want to share His message.

What do you do when you dislike your coworkers or are dissatisfied in your job?

"The LORD will guide you always; He will satisfy your needs in a sun-scorched land and will strengthen your frame. You will be like a well-watered garden, like a spring whose waters never fail." Isaiah 58:11

It is important for you to acknowledge God as your "first boss" rather than man, to remember that God provided your job opportunity, and that you exercised free will when you accepted the opportunity. But perhaps, for whatever reason, you find yourself asking the above question. There are no more job challenges and your inspiration has waned considerably.

Perhaps you've reached a plateau, can't advance any further, feel "stuck" and are thinking of moving on. Perhaps you've outgrown your comfort zone and need to expand beyond your current boundaries because you can no longer create that internal challenge that has kept you going. Generally you feel discouraged, which affects your energy and tolerance in other areas of life as well as your job.

Discontentment is an indication of change and a sign that change is imminent. Barring serious job problems and excluding any grievance procedures, your discontentment most likely stems from internal rather than external factors and expresses itself in a general lack of interest in the job and the people associated with it. General elements of restlessness are present as well.

As we gain life experience and mature, our perspectives change about most aspects of our lives, including our jobs. Once a satisfying and rewarding career, our jobs can become routine, boring, and what to us seems like a waste of time. But we must remember that God put us there for a reason, and doubting our continued purpose can be hard to deal with spiritually as we remain in our present position.

Experiencing feelings of restlessness may mean that you're being called both "from" something and "to" something. Either way, this time in your life can be very disturbing and you need to proceed carefully in all decisions you make. For Christians, this can be a truly difficult time because we want to do what God wants us to do and to follow what we believe is His plan for our life, although certainly no one takes these times lightly.

The restlessness may also mean that the employee is no longer a good "fit" for the job. The job requirements, functions and duties are not ideally suited for your talents, personality, interests, values and skills. It is very common to see people "outgrow" a job.

The best way to prevent positional mismatch is to take a personal assessment of your strengths and weaknesses. Once you are very familiar with your capabilities, you can evaluate a job for potential fit. God gives us each a unique design and wants us to utilize our potential!

When you reach the point that you don't like your coworkers and are dissatisfied with the job as a whole, you need to listen to what God is trying to tell you, to earnestly seek time with Him and to pray for guidance. It may be that a seed was planted in the past and is just now budding. Nevertheless, as you are genuinely discontented with most aspects of your job, it may be time to move in a different direction, and in all probability your reactions indicate this is the time for change. But that means leaving something you're familiar with in search of something new and different and perhaps unknown.

One must watch out for selfish motivation at the root of dissatisfaction. We have counseled quite a few people who want to change jobs JUST for the money, status, or other longing for material goods. As you know, God looks at the heart of an individual. So you want to make sure that your rationale for making a change is pure and upright.

The most common reason clients come to us wanting to make a career transition is that there are too many problems in their current job. People jump ship because they assume "the grass is greener on the other side of the fence." In other words, the perception is that other jobs have fewer problems. Unfortunately, this core belief couldn't be further from the truth. In consulting with hundreds of companies, it's easy to note that they all have about the same amount of problems. They are just different problems in each organization.

Often when anticipating something new is on the horizon, there is a tendency to hit the panic button, but doing that is not the only option available and change need not be a time of upheaval. While you still have your job, you need to exercise control over the negative attitude you have developed to curtail alienating superiors and coworkers. This is a time for patience, with yourself and others, and for self-discipline and strong character to come forth.

If you envision yourself leaving the job, you have the option to do so in a positive manner that demonstrates self-respect as well as respect for others, and to conduct yourself with dignity. There is no need to project your unhappiness onto those who may have no idea of your thoughts, feelings or intentions. If you leave your job because you seek, or feel you are called to, a "higher purpose," don't you think your behavior should reflect those higher goals?

And remember, "change" in the workplace generally takes time to actually happen.

Exercise #6

Questions for Small Group Discussion and / or Personal Reflection

1. When was the last time you got into a disagreement with a coworker or friend?

2. How did you handle the conflict?

3. The next time, in a similar circumstance, how might you change your behavior to come closer to the biblical ideal you may be shooting for?

Activities

1. Select a coworker or associate that you don't particularly get along with. Ask God what you might do to move toward an attitude of reconciliation toward this person.

2. Make a list of your primary work-related strengths and weaknesses. Compare this list with a job description

and what you actually know about the realities of the position. (If you don't have a job description, simply list about six major job functions). Are you in the right position?

How do you know when it's time to move on?

"My son, preserve sound judgment and discernment, do not let them out of your sight; they will be life for you, an ornament to grace your neck." Proverbs 3:21-22

The previous question prepared us for our discussion here by giving clues about needing to make changes. We accept that anxiety is a byproduct of change and that we will experience a myriad of emotions like fear, uncertainty, discontentment, and hope. But God dispels our anxieties and reaffirms our doubts. He encourages us and reassures us.

When God prepares us for change, He puts a restless spirit in our hearts and a conviction that transcends any doubts we may have. While initially we may not recognize this as being from God, when we listen for His voice, read His Word, and know in our hearts that He has a plan for us, we eventually learn to recognize how He communicates with us. He wants us to know the message is from Him, that He needs to speak with us, because we are His instruments helping each other and working toward His greater purpose.

Recently a lady shared her story about making a significant change in her life, a process that took three years to complete and involved her job. She had been at her job for about five years when she began to experience similar circumstances described in the previous question. She had reached a plateau, felt stuck, no longer felt challenged, was suffering negative thoughts about the job in general, and looking for ways to leave. She had no idea of the type of change she would make or when she would make it.

She prayed and talked to God about her presumed "dilemma" and sought direction weekly, if not daily. She relates that during this time she often weighed the positives and negatives of making a change, but that she also experienced a drive to move forward that kept her focused on the future.

Finally, God showed her a way to transition from her job into a new career. Making the change took significant preparation, but refocusing her attention on a new career made her job tolerable until she was able to leave. She began letting go of the old, replacing it with the new.

It was not unusual for her to ask God how long this was all going to take, and she got a big surprise one day while driving to work. When she asked once again about the timing, God said to her, "It's up to you. You've always been free to choose when to leave."

Why did it take this lady three years to make a change? Perhaps because the recent death of her husband and a move just prior to getting that job offered enough of life's challenges. Perhaps in the midst of all that confusion God planted within her a dream in keeping with His further plan for her life.

Everyone experiences circumstances that have the potential to create change. When we listen closely and carefully for God's voice, when we earnestly seek His will for our lives despite our circumstances, when we look to Him for all our needs, He instills within us a sense of who He is. We are called by the Holy Spirit to come unto the Lord and we need to answer the call.

God prepares us and leads us through life events, including getting and leaving a job. He knows the amount of time needed to make a decision that initiates change and allows latitude in that decision, and ultimately He makes His plan for that portion of our lives known.

How will you recognize change and what can you do to be ready when change comes? You need to communicate with God for direction for your life and to be discerning about the choices you make. You need to seek God's counsel frequently and at regular intervals about major issues, such as your job and career.

You also need to be diligent in seeking His timing and to occupy yourself with constructive tasks that promote the positive changes you want or are called to.

Exercise #7

Questions for Small Group Discussion and / or Personal Reflection

1.   What are some of the most difficult changes at work that you have had to deal with in the recent past?

2.   Select one change that you sense God would have you initiate. Begin to sketch an initial plan below.

Activities

Select one work habit that you feel needs to be changed or improved. Document it below.

Describe your change strategy and implement the first step this week.

How do I discover God's will for business decisions and my career?

"So I say to you: Ask and it will be given to you; seek and you will find; knock and the door will be opened to you. For everyone who asks receives; he who seeks finds; and to him who knocks, the door will be opened." Luke 11:9-10

As in the preceding section, the answer to this question is found through prayer and seeking God. When we learn to pray and rely on God to answer our questions and provide for all our needs, we can simply ask Him. He may choose to speak to us via another person, circumstances, or even upon reflecting on nature.

God invites us and wants us to turn to Him in all matters, in all decisions and choices we make, as in which business decisions are best and which career is right for us. Our tendency, however, is to be selective about what we take to Him, as in life and death matters only. If you find yourself reluctant to ask Him about every detail of your life, or if you feel uncomfortable about doing so in any way, you need to find a way through that thinking, to seek those who can help you to see the fullness of God's blessings. Pray with others who can help you break down any barriers you feel. Allow others to intercede for you as you learn to trust God and His Word.

"Trust in the LORD and do good; dwell in the land and enjoy safe pasture. Delight yourself in the LORD and He will give you the desires of your heart." Psalm 37:3-4

When we, as young children, are raised in the Word of God, our tendency to take all our concerns to Him is a natural process. We lovingly and innocently seek His help in almost everything we do. All too often as we continue to grow, however, we stray from our connection with God and as adults frequently lose even more contact. The world has a way of encroaching upon us seemingly without our awareness, which can create havoc if not corrected. Sometimes attempts to reestablish a lost or broken connection with God are painful and take more time, but we must always remember that God loves us.

How do you regain that connectedness with God? Through a simple prayer and asking Him to come into your life again. If you can remember your childhood relationship with Him, then it's like coming home. Once you feel His familiar embrace and His love for you, all boundaries fade away.

You can have your relationship with God for the second, third, or even the first time by simply asking Him to enter your heart and to mend the tear, to remove the barrier that separates you from Him.

Exercise #8

Questions for Small Group Discussion and / or Personal Reflection

1. Describe a decision that you are currently facing.

2. What biblical principles or God-honoring strategies do you want to keep in mind as you deal with the decision described above?

3. How can you involve and seek God in this decision?

Activities

1. Write out an "Action Plan" for what needs to be done in order for you to be pleased with your decision-making process.

2. Jot down a good decision you have made relative to your work in recent memory.

3.   Pray about a decision you need to make in the future. Ask God for wisdom regularly with respect to this issue. Write down the insights you receive in your day timer or journal.

How can I incorporate prayer in the middle of the day? I know I need God's help on phone calls, with meetings and projects.

"Trust in the LORD with all your heart and lean not on your own understanding; in all your ways acknowledge Him, and He will make your paths straight." Proverbs 3:5-6

Today's general work environment is replete with policies and procedures on every aspect of running a business, including statements regarding the number and length of breaks employees are to have daily. These designated times as well as other breaks, such as mealtimes, offer ideal opportunities to speak with God on any aspect of your business agenda. However, you can speak with Him at "unscheduled" times as well. He wants you to present all your concerns to Him, to develop a dialogue with Him on a regular basis, and to offer you guidance in every part of your life.

"But," you say, "I just don't feel comfortable praying at work. What if someone catches me? What then? How am I going to explain this?"

Which is stronger: your need to talk to God, or worrying about any embarrassment you might experience?

Christians talk to God. Period. And, yes, sometimes you will be nervous about doing that, but your emotional state should never prevent you from doing what, for many Christians, is a very natural and spontaneous act. Why? Because God is here for you and can help you. Never be hesitant to take your concerns to The One with the answers.

Your prayer time with God is generally private, regardless of how many others are around you, and there is never an inappropriate time to pray, despite your full agenda. Finding time is simply a matter of silently making your concerns known to God. He is ready to help you, even in a short prayer before a phone call or a meeting, to give you the right words for the situation.

Frequent prayer helps to keep prayer simple. As you become more comfortable with your prayer life, you'll find that your "access to God" improves as well. Why? Because you are learning to break down barriers that keep you from Him, and when you make God a priority in your life, finding time to talk with Him is as natural as breath itself.

Through prayer and supplication make your needs known to God. He has all the answers and is available anytime. Develop a daily habit to pray about all matters and do it as many times as you need to. God is not only your boss—He is your best friend. Talking with Him is good for your soul.

Exercise #9

Questions for Small Group Discussion and / or Personal Reflection

Describe how you might be able to incorporate prayer as a regular part of your normal work routine.

When do you think would be some of the most important times during the workday to pray (for example, before an important meeting or phone call)?

Activities

Take a prayer walk at some point during your next workday. This can be done by offering a short prayer on your way down the hall, during a break or at some point where you can take a break from the hectic day-to-day pressures.

Write down the different types of people you encounter during an average week (such as a boss, coworkers, clients, vendors, competitors). Find a place that is easily visible on your desk and place some type of reminder that will help you remember to pray for these people God has allowed to enter your life.

If Jesus Christ is my "Real" Boss, how come I don't sense His presence and power?

"One of them, an expert in the law, tested him with this question: 'Teacher, which is the greatest commandment in the Law?' Jesus replied: 'Love the Lord your God with all your heart and with all your soul and with all your mind.' This is the first and greatest commandment." Matthew 22:35-38

The world has many distractions that interfere with our communication with God. It takes our concerted effort to maintain a clear pathway that keeps the channels open. When we feel distanced from God, we experience confusion and life takes on a less ordered and sane dimension. It is our Christian privilege to seek God's will in all that we do, so it is essential that we find our way back to Him.

When we sense the absence of His presence and power, it means that we have allowed other items to come before God and have given them priority over Him. This can happen gradually without much thought on our part, and therein lies a key to why we no longer sense He is with us: a lack of conscious thought and intent to include Him in our life. We become so busy with the duties and problems of living that we allow God to be pushed aside.

He wants us to enjoy our lives and to help us solve problems, but He also wants us to place Him before everything else in life and has given specific instructions.

When we feel distance in our relationship with God, with His Son Jesus, we need to seriously look at exactly where we have placed Him in our life. And we need to repair the connection that we allowed to break our communication with Him. How do we do this? All we have to do is ask in a simple prayer:

"Father, I come to you at this time thankful for the blessings you have given me. Lord Jesus, I have been away from you and want to return. I need your guidance for my life. I need to feel your love and acceptance again. I ask your forgiveness for my sins. Thank you, Lord, for your gift of salvation and for loving me. I petition these requests in Jesus' name and for thy glory and in the name of thy love. Amen."

Prayer is the roadmap back to an intimate relationship with God. It repairs the broken connection each time we break it. You can begin now with the simple prayer above to again feel God's presence and power in your life. Renew those activities, those thoughts and gestures that helped you feel connected with God: prayer; being with other Christians; church services and participation in its activities; volunteering to help others; extensions of kindness and support to those in need; taking the time to pray for or with a friend or stranger.

Pray and give of yourself, your talents, the gifts God has given only to you. He gave them to you for His reasons and He wants you to share the fruit of His Spirit with others: love, joy, peace, patience, kind-ness, goodness, faithfulness, gentleness and self-control. **(Galatians 5:22-23)**

Exercise #10

Questions for Small Group Discussion and / or Personal Reflection

1. Describe how close you feel to God right now. What thoughts and feelings come to mind?

2. Pinpoint one or two barriers that might be inhibiting a closer relationship with the Lord.

3. How could you address these barriers in a positive and constructive manner?

Activities

In prayer, ask God to allow you to experience, by the power of His Holy Spirit, the fruit of the Spirit. This includes love, joy, peace, patience, kindness, goodness, faithfulness, gentleness and self-control.

Reflect on habits you may have unconsciously developed that make it difficult to experience the presence and power of God. Write a few action steps on how you could change one negative habit that you feel might be getting in the way of being closer to God.

I see this huge gap between my faith on Sunday morning and the "real world" Monday through Sunday. I don't want to make work a "Sunday School" class, but still I need some practical tips to make my faith stronger throughout each day.

"Therefore, my dear brothers, stand firm. Let nothing move you. Always give yourselves fully to the work of the Lord, because you know that your labor in the Lord is not in vain." 1 Corinthians 15:58

The transition from Sunday worship to Monday's "real world" situations can certainly dampen Sunday's soul-enriching message. But—you either have faith or you don't have faith. You either practice your faith or allow it to slide into a place of less prominence. Again, this can easily happen once we reenter Monday's work world.

God tells us to hold fast to His Word in order to perform the work we do for Him. We are to remain strong in our faith, and we can turn to prayer and ask God to strengthen us so that we remain an instrument for His work. The reading and hearing of His Word strengthens us and adds security to our workweek.

Here are five practical ways we suggest to strengthen your faith:

1.   Talking to God in daily prayer about every aspect

of your life is the most practical way to keep your faith strong. Prayer is the easiest way to keep your communication with God functioning properly and it brings direction and peace in life. There are no limits when it comes to how often or under what circumstances you should pray, so develop a routine of frequent prayer in all matters. Talk to God as you do to others who cross your path daily, expressing your needs, wants, frustrations, desires and dreams in simple terms.

2.   Gain strength from prayer and then share your faith by expressing it openly to others in kindness, gentleness, and with a spirit of love, joy and peace. Doing so helps to recall the Sunday morning blessings you received.

3.   Create a habit of doing good deeds throughout your workweek. Volunteer your time, energy and resources to help others. Ask God to place you where you need to be to get His work done, reaching out to others in practical ways that assist them, whether through scheduled or unscheduled events. Taking major steps and thinking you need to do sometimes "big" is not always part of God's plan.

4.   God has given us work to serve Him, other people and us. With respect to serving God on the job, it is interesting to note that the words "work" and "worship" mean the same thing in the original language of the Old Testament (Hebrew). So, we go to work to bring honor and glory to God, to identify and meet the needs of those we can serve AND to get our own needs met (income, sense of pride in workmanship, etc.). Go to work for the same reasons as you would go to church. The barrier between the two must be broken.

5. And certainly, with every opportunity available, tell others about Jesus and how He IS the Light in your life. At every opportunity share your faith with others. Doing so will sometimes mean taking a tenuous step on your part, but dare to take that step. You don't know what the other person needs, but God does. Ask Him, when in doubt, to give you the words that person needs to hear. Listen closely, because it may be one simple word, or many. Be sensitive to the other person's circumstances as you share God's Word from your heart.

Regularly enriching your soul with the Word of God and working for Him will sustain you in whatever situation you find yourself, regardless of the day of the week. Look inside your heart to find the wellspring of joy and hope God placed within you and share your gifts with others. And remember to smile often and let God's Light radiate from you.

Exercise #11

Questions for Small Group Discussion and / or Personal Reflection

What is it like for you to incorporate your "Sunday Faith" into your "Monday Vocation"?

What is one thing that you can do to carry over the spiritual highs of church and ministry involvement over the weekend to the workweek?

Activity

Find a scripture that directly relates to the challenges and / or opportunities you face at work. (A concordance at the back of most bibles can help you find passages by category). Jot down that scripture on a 3 x 5 card and put it in your car. Read it (and preferably meditate on it) as you drive to and from work. Try this for a few days and see what impact this activity has on your attitude and actions.

Secondary Home and Family Concerns

How can I balance work and family life?

"Teach me your way, O LORD, and I will walk in your truth; give me an undivided heart, that I may fear your name." Psalm 86:11

This problem has become widespread among the Christian community and is not limited to Christian homes. Today in many two-parent households, the workforce claims both parents who frequently work in schedules that overlap. If not checked and watched carefully, the chaos that erupts can have devastating effects on everyone in the home. As the general pace of today's job market has increased, the demands on home and family have not only increased but narrowed windows of actual time that would normally be divided more equally. The tendency for families to split into sections rather than to function as a unit is evident in talking with people on the job, at social events, or even strangers on the street.

With two priorities—home and work—meeting the responsibilities of each keeps most families busier than they would like to be. Life offers excessive amounts of stimulation on a daily basis, and when either one or both partners work, especially outside the home, it becomes more difficult to reach an equitable compromise of how to spend the necessary time at work and still meet family needs and commitments.

Trying to meet dual life demands often leaves families feeling unbalanced. Once life becomes unbalanced we lose focus, which, in turn, affects our peace. When our focus is blurred and peace succumbs to anxiety, it's only a few short steps to chaos.

At all times and in everything you do or approach in life, putting God first is your top priority. Even when you place God at the center of your life, life will still present moments that try you and tend to pull you apart. But you must keep Him as the center of life always and seek His guidance. Keeping God first and the renewing of His Word in your spirit brings peace.

"Peace I leave with you; my peace I give you. I do not give to you as the world gives. Do not let your hearts be troubled and do not be afraid." John 14:27

Here are seven practical steps you can take to help balance work and family life:

1. Create and maintain a written or electronic work schedule and use it each day on the job. Try as much as possible to stay within those time commitments. An occasional exception is to be expected but need not be disruptive.

2. Keep a home schedule with everyone's activities listed. As much as possible support each other as a group and make certain no member is left unsupported in any activity.

3. Share as many family meals together as possible during the workweek. If nightly gatherings are not possible, commit to a specific number of meals together and consider sharing or alternating meal preparation by family members, either individually or in teams. (You will need to establish and keep a "come home time" in order to faithfully honor commitments in the evening.)

4. Make a date with your partner on a regular basis, if

not weekly then as frequently as possible, but make a commitment and keep it.

5. Pray together as a family. Sharing prayer rotation during family meals brings family members together and promotes harmony. Also feel free to share the highs and lows of your day. In this way the spouse and children get to see and hear what work life is really like.

6. Be willing to spend quiet time together as a family— reading, hobbies, homework or games—where each member can enjoy an individual interest. Everyone appreciates quality time together, regardless of the activity, and it is not always necessary to have a group activity going.

7. Take the time to offer concerted prayer for each family member on the commute home. Take a break from dwelling on the mistakes of the day.

God wants your life to have balance in all areas so that He can fulfill His purpose through you, and when you are out of balance in any area, just ask Him how to restore it. Perhaps you need to slow the pace down just a little in order to know Him and to hear Him better.

Exercise #12

Questions for Small Group Discussion and / or Personal Reflection

1. How satisfied are you with the time you are currently investing in each of the important areas of your life? Work? Personal? Community? Church? Family?

2. What are the most significant barriers you face in trying to balance your time?

3. What is one thing you can do this week to simplify your life in order to make room for activities of higher importance?

Activities

1. Keep a daily journal for one week. In it record each activity you engage in (by 15 minute increments). This exercise may seem tedious at first, but you'll be amazed at how the results demonstrate just where and how you really are spending your time, versus your desired time utilization.

2. Pray over your schedule. Ask God to reveal priorities you need to change and affirm areas in which you are making commendable progress.

My job has become a wedge between my spouse and me. It's the enemy.

"When you go into battle in your own land against an enemy who is oppressing you, sound a blast on the trumpets. Then you will be remembered by the LORD your God and rescued from your enemies."
Numbers 10:9

The job is not the enemy. Satan is the enemy who has stolen your time and focus. He has invaded your mind and distracted you from who and what is important in your life. Most importantly, he has distracted you from God, and by doing so has opened doors to further mistrust of ideas, people and principles you hold dear.

When this type of thinking is prevalent in your life, you operate with a distorted view that has the potential to destroy the relationships you desperately want to hold on to. Once you allow this type of thinking to grip your mind, it's easy to blame a job, a spouse, or a third party for what is going wrong in your life, and consequences exist for potentially irrevocable damage that can leave families with emotional scars, some of which last for many painful years.

There are many influences on a person's balance of marriage and work. Unfortunately, some influences will inevitably end up as wedges in the marital relationship, regardless of how solid you think your marriage is or how dedicated you are to your job. Seemingly innocent distractions at work, such as another person paying more attention to you (or to your spouse), can be misinterpreted and erupt into falsehoods that spell disaster.

How does this disruption happen? The amount of time spent on the job, including daily preparation and travel, is often greater than actual time spent with spouse and family. When coworkers share extended periods of time and get along well with each other, it's natural that they may form deeper bonds than casual friendship. Add other influences, such as coworkers sharing a common bond of meeting work challenges, or flirting, and suddenly you can find yourself in a breeding ground of marital distrust.

Why does this disruption happen? After repeated times of spousal separation due to job-related issues/responsibilities, the partner who is left alone (or left out) is the one who most often begins to feel insecure and, consequently, blames the job rather than the other person. So, while one partner is getting needs met and may not be aware of a potential troubling situation, the other partner frequently experiences separation on a deeper level and accompanying anxiety that can form quickly.

The emotional tendency is to experience anxiety first as fear of separation and then as fear of loss of a loved one, which can cause extreme emotional upset. These feelings are seldom easily put into words and may take the form of domestic arguments or spats in an undercurrent of mistrust and fear.

Because the balance between work and home can be a delicate one, we caution you to never take either situation for granted and to be mindful of your role in all of your relationships.

How do you remove the disruptive wedge, correct your thinking in these situations, and get back on track? First you pray and ask God for help.

"Do not be anxious about anything, but in everything, by prayer and petition, with thanksgiving, present your requests to God." Philippians 4:6

Then you stop the "blame game" and honestly look at the job and your relationship with your spouse. You need to have open communication with both your boss and your spouse to clear up misconceptions, questions and confusion. You also need to ask yourself how you may have contributed to the fear that grips you.

Remember, misunderstandings are breeding grounds for confusion and mistrust, and a mind clouded from the truth tends to panic, which creates more chaos.

In seeking answers to resolve problems in these areas, you must be willing to speak to the issues directly with sincerity in your words and honor from your heart to find the truth. You must be willing to review and regain control of your responsibilities to your job and your spouse, and to forgive yourself and others for any misunderstandings or false accusations.

> "And when you stand praying, if you hold anything against anyone, forgive him, so that your Father in heaven may forgive you your sins." Mark 11:25-26

While the truth may not always be what you want to hear, there can be no replacement for it. Truth lights the way to eternal life.

> "Jesus answered, "I am the way and the truth and the life. No one comes to the Father except through me." John 14:6

It takes forgiving hearts to withstand the mental and emotional pain troublesome situations can bring. But you can gain strength through prayer and faith that God will lead you through difficult times, and that Satan, although he may appear in many disguises, loses when you call on the name of Jesus.

Exercise #13

Questions for Small Group Discussion and / or Personal Reflection

Where might you be playing the "Blame Game" in your life?

Jot down one area of your life in which you have (most likely unknowingly) given away responsibility, when this activity is really within your control.

How might you be looking at your job as "The Enemy"?

Describe an action step or change in core belief that you need to make in order for you to convert "The Enemy" to "A Friend."

Activities

1.   Make a list of the battles you seem to be fighting on a regular basis.

2. Select one battle you want to fight. Write down your strategy in a journal or other place where you can reflect on it regularly.

How do you build any kind of marital relationship when both spouses work outside the home (which is 90% of the cases)?

"He will be the sure foundation for your times, a rich store of salvation and wisdom and knowledge; the fear of the LORD is the key to this treasure." Isaiah 33:6

What we're talking about here is a foundation for a marital relationship that can withstand any changes a couple might encounter, and change in marriage, as in life, is guaranteed. The foundation needs to be as strong as a couple can possibly make it when planning a life together. An important key to remember is that with marriage the "two" become more important than the "one." Compromise is expected in marriage and couples need to know beforehand how they will react and what they will do when situations arise that tend to separate them.

Marriage transforms two people from "I" to "We" when the second "I do" is spoken. What may be considered an old-fashioned idea in today's modern and sophisticated society has merits: that two people get to know one another before they say "I do" and commit to a lifelong relationship.

Couples need time to share their likes and dislikes, habits, preferences and beliefs regarding ideas, principles and faith. They need to discuss every aspect of their pending lives together, including family and children, careers and finances, and how they will deal with sickness, phase of life changes, and the death of loved ones and each other.

ckquote То

Unfortunately, many couples never take time to share these important moments and parts of themselves. Rather, in their hurry to make a commitment, they take things for granted, make assumptions, and fail to ask questions for fear of upsetting the course of events they have so often hastily mapped out for themselves. They tend to hold in reserve the essence of who they are for fear of losing the other person. This is more human nature than deception, generally a subconscious process they're not even aware is taking place within them.

The current question is a good example of how couples can find distance between them. In today's liberal and tolerant society where people tend to "do their own thing" to the exclusion of others, couples can find themselves caught up in the hectic routine of work, just trying to make a living, and end up trapped in demands on their time and energy. When they compromise time with their spouse, they feel a loss of the other, can begin to grieve, and naturally seek to regain what they sense they are losing. It takes a strong commitment to each other and to the principles they have set for their marriage to work through conflicting circumstances.

God puts us in pairs, combining the strengths of each to better do His work. Christian couples particularly tend to feel and sense that they are "complete" in marriage because God has brought them together. The greatest strength a couple can have is to keep His first commandment.

> "Jesus replied: 'Love the Lord your God with all your heart and with all your soul and with all your mind.' This is the first and greatest commandment." Matthew 22:37-38

When both spouses work outside the home, it takes planning and commitment by both partners to uphold keeping their marital relationship a priority over work demands. Remembering and incorporating fun and interesting experiences of their dating into their marital routine eases stress due to work situations. Acts of thoughtfulness toward each other help to ease one's load and are a reminder that their mutual support is intact.

Spouses need to keep the lines of communication fully open on all matters that concern their lives. It's not necessary to know every detail, but taking an occasional "pulse check" to clarify and disseminate confusion, frustration, and generally clear the air provides a chance for reaffirmation that they are on the same track, that their goals and ideas are compatible and in sync with each other. God wants couples to be supportive, considerate and kind toward one another.

> "Therefore, as God's chosen people, holy and dearly loved, clothe yourselves with compassion, kindness, humility, gentleness and patience. Bear with each other and forgive whatever grievances you may have against one another. Forgive as the Lord forgave you."
> Colossians 3:12-13

Exercise #14

Questions for Small Group Discussion and / or Personal Reflection

1. What do you think your spouse, or close friend, likes most about their job?

2. What do you think your spouse, or close friend, dislikes most about their job?

3. What do you need from those nearest to you in order to feel more supported?

Activities

1. If married, go out on a date and discuss how each of you feels about your job. Furthermore, ask him or her what you could do to create a closer "partnership" in your work.

2. Discuss with your spouse what frustrations you have relative to your vocation and your relationship to him or her. For example, discuss what are the stressors, frustrations, financial issues, unmet aspirations or pressures you are feeling.

3. Discuss with your mate how you can divide up the responsibilities at home in order to best accommodate the demands of a career and schedule therein.

4. Devise a plan for how you can better support each other in each of your respective jobs. Review these goals and action steps on Sunday evenings for a few weeks. Discuss your progress.

General Life Issues

I experience tremendous stress each day. How can my faith practically help me here?

"Do not conform any longer to the pattern of this world, but be transformed by the renewing of your mind. Then you will be able to test and approve what God's will is—His good, pleasing and perfect will."
Romans 12:2

Stress is an invasive element that insidiously creeps into our daily lives stripping us of having a sense of control over life. Our society is bombarded with an endless stream of messages to add more adventure, excitement and thrills to our lives and to compete for something that always seems to be "out there" somewhere. The residual effects we experience from this barrage of stimulation stem in part from the very excitement present in commercials and general advertising we are exposed to daily.

From observation alone it seems that television commercials have become shorter but have multiplied in numbers. After the average consumer has been exposed to approximately 20 different advertising items in a 30-minute program, we can readily understand why we feel as though we've ridden a roller coaster of mass confusion. Our minds, our psyches, simply become overwhelmed.

Further, we attend high-power meetings, seminars and workshops with even greater exposure to excessive stimulation. Our home and volunteer activities can get out of hand to the point that there is a sense we are losing or have lost control. Eventually our minds, emotions and psyches begin to shut down as a result of these high volumes of provocative information and excessive activity. We simply cannot take overload on a consistent basis without suffering consequences on many levels.

Consciously or subconsciously we reach a peak of saturation that affects us physiologically in any number of ways:

1. Our pulse quickens and blood pressure often rises.
2. We tend to eat more or less but certainly erratically.
3. We lose sleep or develop some sort of sleep problem.
4. Our biorhythms become confused, our electrolytes unbalanced, and our electrical mechanisms begin to misfire.
5. We begin to experience malaise or some physical symptoms or illness.

On an emotional level we can become moody, angry, out-of-sorts, depressed, argumentative, and generally feel like we're walking a tightrope and about to lose our footing. Often it is others who notice these changes first, our spouse or those around us on a regular basis, such as coworkers. If we're lucky, some may care enough to alert us to subtle changes that are taking place: "Jeff, have you been working late too many nights, buddy? You seem extra tired these days. Are you getting enough rest? Is there anything I can do to help?"

From a spiritual standpoint, when mental confusion combines with physical depletion, daily prayer may get pushed aside due to a creeping and prevailing sense of depression that affects our ability to function. Or the reverse may happen, where prayer becomes more frequent but loses its sincerity and purpose. Routine faith participation, such as involvement in church activities, may decline as well.

When Christians stop taking their concerns to God, there is a sense that God has abandoned them and that life is shutting down. In extreme situations, believers begin to question their faith, which precipitates deeper depression and even withdrawal from life. People who do not know God or have a faith concept suffer incredible pain.

But you don't have to fall victim to life's "worldliness." You have a choice to live a saner, more organized life based on the principles of God's teachings. The Bible is replete with guidelines for living a balanced life, and there are many faith-based resources in psychology, health and philosophy to help reduce personal, business and cultural stressors. These resources can be found in bookstores and on Christian websites by entering a keyword or phrase such as "Christian teachings" into a search engine such as Google.

It is essential that you find ways to release your "pressure valve" in order to maintain intellectual, physical, emotional and spiritual stability throughout life. Living your faith by reading the Bible, unselfishly helping and doing for others, communing with God on a regular basis and taking ALL of your concerns to Him bring a tremendous amount of peace to life.

We are to seek God's Word in all things. The Scriptures provide many clues to avoiding a chaotic lifestyle and give reassurance.

"Do not store up for yourselves treasures on earth, where moth and rust destroy, and where thieves break in and steal. But store up for yourselves treasures in heaven, where moth and rust do not destroy, and where thieves do not break in and steal. For where your treasure is, there your heart will be also." Matthew 6:19-21

"Great peace have they who love your law, and nothing can make them stumble." Psalm 119:165

Exercise #15

Questions for Small Group Discussion and / or Personal Reflection

1. What is causing the most stress in your work and home life?

2. What have you tried to implement to deal with the stress that has not been working? Why do you think you keep trying to manage your stress level with strategies that aren't working?

3. If you want different and better results for your future, you must stop the ineffective methods of the past. Furthermore, you need to select new ways to deal with the difficulties of life in order to make proactive changes. What is one change you would like to make in order to better manage stress in your life?

Activity

Select one way to release your "Pressure Valve." Try this action step to see if it helps. If not, try another strategy until you find an action that does work.

What kind of spiritual warfare am I likely to encounter in a secular marketplace and how should I handle it?

"The Lord will rescue me from every evil attack and will bring me safely to His heavenly kingdom. To Him be glory for ever and ever. Amen." 2 Timothy 4:18

Situations of spiritual warfare surround us every day of our lives, in and out of the marketplace, and come in many forms: telling lies, gossip, false accusations, creating ideas of false competition and/or rivalry, making one doubt one's abilities. The aim of spiritual warfare is to create confusion, to pit people against God and against each other with the use of mind games and deception.

Being subject to daily battles against enemies we cannot see, we can know they are present whenever we feel (sense) that something is not right. Even when we fail to recognize the signs or don't fully understand the circumstances, we often know we are faced with an enemy that wants to take from us, to destroy us and leave us destitute in as many areas of life as possible.

How do we know? We experience anxiety and doubt, a feeling of foreboding, and have an innate sense of something being taken from us, and that puts us on guard.

To combat these warring situations takes our watchful attention to life and diligent efforts to stand firm in their midst. As we grow in our relationship with God, learn to know Him and what He teaches for our lives, we gain strength to fight battles. From His Word we learn there is victory.

"For the LORD your God is the one who goes with you to fight for you against your enemies to give you victory." Deuteronomy 20:4

When you find yourself in spiritual warfare, or sense that you are involved in a spiritual battle, pray immediately for deliverance from harm. Call on the name of the Lord to protect you and to give you courage in adversity. Handle the situation with honest words, a pure heart, and avoid getting trapped in a web of deceit. Remember, Jesus is the Way, the Truth and the Life. **(John 14:6)**

Put on the full amour of God **(Ephesians 6:11)**. Along with prayer, study His Word. Develop your "sixth sense" which will guide you away from trouble. Listen to that small voice inside your head, inside your heart, your soul that warns you when something is not right. It is there to protect you, to keep you safe. Talk to God about all that causes you to feel fearful and without peace. **(See Ephesians 6:12-20** for a complete strategy for victory.)

Exercise #16

Questions for Small Group Discussion and / or Personal Reflection

1. What forms of spiritual warfare are you most likely to encounter more frequently than others?

2. What is your natural reaction to being spiritually attacked? Is this a reaction tendency that occurs regularly?

3. How do you think God wants you to respond when the enemy strikes next in a similar situation?

Activities

Ask God to reveal to you schemes that the evil one may be trying to employ to get you off track with God. Prayerfully, put on your spiritual armor and fight your battle in the spiritual realm.

Ask God to reveal to you the name and circumstances around a brother or sister in Christ who may be under Satan's attack. Come against the tempter and accuser with the Truth of God that speaks directly to the circumstances occurring. Claim victory, by the blood of Jesus Christ.

How do I cope with failure, setbacks and trials?

"In this you greatly rejoice, though now for a little while you may have had to suffer grief in all kinds of trials. These have come so that your faith—of greater worth than gold, which perishes even though refined by fire—may be proved genuine and may result in praise, glory and honor when Jesus Christ is revealed."
1 Peter 1:6-7

We all experience failure, setbacks and trials in life. Our reactions to these situations determine whether we use them as positive or negative life experiences, thus setting the stage for our reactions to more troubled times that will surely come. God allows us to go through diverse situations to prepare us for even tougher times ahead so that we may more effectively fight battles to His glory. It is our responsibility to learn from these times and to grow intellectually, emotionally and spiritually.

When such events happen, ask God for and trust Him to give you insight into the situation and to put people in your life who will help lead you through difficult times. Be forthcoming to ask specific questions and be willing to look at the entire experience, and within yourself, for clues of what happened and why.

While some of these challenging events and times will have less of an impact on us and/or our loved ones than others (what happens to those we love and care about also affects us), they all offer valuable lessons designed to help us through life so that we may learn from them, live life more abundantly, and help others.

As human beings we suffer illnesses, physical and emotional pain, and disappointments. We experience emotional highs and lows, and most of us will experience both great elation and the depths of despair at some point in our lifetime, either directly or indirectly through loved ones. If we are without God, our soul aches and we experience emotional and spiritual death. In extreme cases, physical death occurs through suicide or less obvious causes, such as complications of neglect and loneliness. Some people simply give up on life.

As Christians it pains us to see others who do not have a relationship with God, and we share the pain they experience. Our souls reach out to them to offer comfort.

We need to be active participants in our own lives and to take responsibility for our thoughts and actions. We need to live life from points of strength as God intended us to through His Word, and to persevere rather than live in fear and doubt. When we are strong and know that God is the center of our life, we need to reach out to others less strong and less committed in their faith, to offer help and to share the gifts and guidance God has given to us. It's important to keep a positive attitude about life and to turn to God for guidance in all matters.

In closing Part I, we look to God's Word that tells who we are and His direction for our lives.

> "You are the light of the world. A city on a hill cannot be hidden. Neither do people light a lamp and put it under a bowl. Instead they put it on its stand, and it gives light to everyone in the house. In the same way, let your light shine before men, that they may see your good deeds and praise your Father in heaven."
> Matthew 5:14-16

Here are six keys to coping with setbacks:

T: Trust God for strength to endure.

R: Remember God's previous faithfulness.

I: Implore God for help in the midst of it all.

A: Ask wise people for advice.

L: Leave the future to God.

S: Seek character, change NOT just "relief."

Exercise #17

Questions for Small Group Discussion and / or Personal Reflection

1. What are the setbacks, fears and/or trials you have been facing lately?

2. Which problem is causing you to worry the most?

3. What could you do to initiate positive change in this area of your life, with God's help?

Activity

Before retiring for the evening tonight, share with God the concerns that are uppermost in your mind. You may just want to have a simple time of prayer and ask God to take control of your situation. Place your trust and dependency on Him for peace and sovereign answers.

PART II

Counseling Career Issues

This section presents real career-related issues that clients face. The scenarios are extracted from actual cases and names are withheld in keeping with confidentiality requirements. In some accounts, the main facts have been augmented with helpful elaboration and additional details to parallel issues faced by the general readership, yet the core facts of each scenario are representative of common challenges that clients encounter.

The cases presented offer no guarantees, as individual cases may differ greatly, yet each scenario represents an outcome of what may be typically experienced. Outcomes have been documented where actual results were positive, negative or "in process." The accounts are structured to offer greater awareness of general principles to follow in learning about issues and to applying important points to a specific situation.

Our purpose for sharing a wide variety of cases and outcomes is manifold. First, we trust that by learning about difficulties others face, you may feel less alone in your own plight. Many of the problems discussed are common to more people than you might think and why we selected these particular cases. Reading about them will give you a glimpse into the unfortunate and sometimes tragic circumstances many people face, and although details may vary, general trends are present.

Second, it is our prayer that you will see a pattern emerge

as we address each issue. Faith in God and biblically based solutions is the true path by which we discover answers to personal struggles. Discovering this secret to successful living will help you move to a new level of faith.

Third, we trust that by reading these accounts you will come to a fresh understanding of how your spiritual life is intertwined with your work life. We believe you will gain a fresh perspective about your own career, one that is filled with a new sense of gratitude for the vocational blessings you have.

You will read of instances where clients have victoriously applied their faith to career problems and realized extremely positive results. However, not all clients have experienced tremendous life change. Some remain "in process," still dealing with personal challenges. As real life shows us daily, recovery and implementing a new direction takes longer for some folks than others.

A common theme in all scenarios is that, generally speaking, successful career transition journeys and the corresponding trials associated with them are most effectively addressed through personal faith, applying biblical principles, and the appropriating promises of God.

Now let us continue our discussion by looking at the nine career issues cited at the beginning of our book. We will approach them from both a practical and a biblical perspective and examine the specific ways we helped these clients to deal with their career issues.

A recently divorced parent sleeping in a one-room apartment with three kids needs to take a job at McDonald's to show responsibility for child support.

"I cry to you, O LORD; I say, 'You are my refuge, my portion in the land of the living.' Listen to my cry, for I am in desperate need; rescue me from those who pursue me, for they are too strong for me. Set me free from my prison, that I may praise your name. Then the righteous will gather about me because of your goodness to me." Psalm 142:5-7

In an ugly divorce between two young parents that also involved child custody, the husband had alleged the mother's neglect of their three children and wanted them removed from her care. However, lacking evidence to support his allegations, the court cautiously awarded temporary custody to the mother with stipulation that Child Protective Services review the case, and that the unemployed mother obtain employment in order to keep the children. A review court date was set for 60 days, at which time the court would make its final decision.

As a devout Christian, the mother had placed her trust in God to provide for the family's needs and to keep the children with her, vehemently denying any charges of neglect. When she originally came to us for career guidance, she was feeling anxious and desperate about her circumstances, which had prompted her to accept a part-time job as a McDonald's cashier just one day after the court hearing.

In choosing a path to assume responsibility, this parent's actions clearly demonstrated to us a commitment to do whatever was necessary to provide for her family, to maintain custody of her children, and to keep the family intact as much as possible under the circumstances. When we looked more closely at her capabilities, we found that her work history included a prior position as an office worker for a major firm in another city.

We initially helped this young mother to put recent events in perspective and thus reduce her anxieties, as she continued to work for the first time since her last child's birth the previous year. With some encouragement, she decided to apply for a more responsible position with a company that paid better wages and offered more time to spend with her young children. Fortunately, family members were able to help with their care while she worked as cashier and also pursued job interviews.

The incentive to keep her children inspired this mother to persevere in her efforts to support herself and further develop her vocational talents, and in time she gained greater strength in her abilities to meet new life demands. Just two days prior to the review court date, she secured full-time employment with a local company as a managerial staff assistant.

At the follow-up court appearance, she was able to satisfactorily demonstrate to the court that she was capable of providing for her family. The CPS reported the child neglect charges to be unfounded. That, along with the mother's new position, making more money and also providing the necessary care for her young children, influenced the court to award her joint custody with her as the custodial parent.

Exercise #18

Questions for Small Group Discussion and / or Personal Reflection

1. Have you ever experienced a period of financial or other type of poverty where your very existence was a struggle each day? Write it down below.

2. How do you think God wants us to deal with periods of difficult circumstances like the mother described in this scenario? Jot down your thoughts below.

Activity

In prayer, ask God to reveal someone to you who is less fortunate in some way. What is one thing you could do that would bring honor and glory to God as well as serve this individual? Commit to initiate whatever actions He brings to mind.

A laid-off executive is so fearful of lack of employment that he makes 70 networking visits in his first 7 weeks. (This is more than most clients will do in 6 months.)

"Humble yourselves, therefore, under God's mighty hand, that He may lift you up in due time. Cast all your anxiety on Him because He cares for you. Your enemy the devil prowls around like a roaring lion looking for someone to devour."
1 Peter 5:6-8

When sudden, unexpected, or even planned layoff happens at any level, the amount of disruption and confusion that enters a person's life can be overwhelming, particularly to sozmeone who felt very secure in their position. In looking for new employment, people often fail to recall the diversity of work experience they gain over time and forget essential contributions they have made to the workforce in general, a tendency of those who seek career counseling. This 45-year-old client was no exception in failing to recall his total attributes.

Our support in this situation was to diffuse our client's anxiety as a result of being laid off, and to help him look at his resume over his entire career rather than strictly based on his last job. Without realizing it, he had neglected other significant work attributes that we detected once we talked with him at length.

When asked why he had so diligently sought employment,

he admitted that he had not realized how closely identified he had become with his last job, an executive position he had held for almost 15 years of his 25 years of service. He had gained a degree of status, which he enjoyed and which was hard for him to relinquish, and felt he must make a lateral move to regain his positive self-image.

Despite having a network of friends and associates, being "out in the cold looking for a job," as he put it, produced severe anxiety that he was no longer the man he thought himself to be. He identified himself as a man of faith and believed that God would help him to deal with thoughts and feelings of self-doubt. His support network was indeed strong.

On the surface, it appears this executive is overextending himself in the amount of effort he put forth to find employment. However, it is this energy and effort that helped him to become an executive—backed, no doubt, by strong patterns of self-discipline and focus. Despite his unfortunate circumstances and in the face of adversity, he continued to exert the drive necessary in seeking to secure another position.

This gentleman's aggressive approach to tackling unemployment was for him a natural way of doing business. His repeated patterns in thought and behavior had become habits that were extremely difficult to change. This case demonstrates that basic patterns practiced over time tend to remain with us, especially as we age.

At our last interview this gentleman was still unemployed, but stated that his self-doubts had been replaced with renewed self-confidence, and that rather than seek employment with someone else, he was considering starting his own business with previous employees who also lost their jobs.

Exercise #19

Questions for Small Group Discussion and / or Personal Reflection

When do you tend to be most anxious or fearful that you may lose your job?

To what extent is your job the primary source of your personal identity, self-worth and self-image?

Do you feel secure and stable in your employment? Why or why not?

Activity

In prayer, ask God to help you identify areas of your career or job transition where you may be over-extending yourself, feel driven, and are too concerned about potential employment adversity.

A gentleman has no support from his spouse. She comments upon seeing him at the computer, "At least you're doing something productive now."

"Therefore, as God's chosen people, holy and dearly loved, clothe yourselves with compassion, kindness, humility, gentleness and patience. Bear with each other and forgive whatever grievances you may have against one another. Forgive as the Lord forgave you." Colossians 3:12-13

Judging others is an undesirable human characteristic, but one that we all possess. Criticisms are often directed toward those we love or are closely tied to in some way, as in marriage. Frequently, they are a result of extreme frustration on some level rather than a mean character. Nevertheless, when uttered without thought, or with intention, it is easy for the target of unkind words to feel attacked and unsupported.

In stressful situations husbands and wives sometimes unwittingly display disregard for the other person's feelings when they make flippant and hurtful comments. Often the spouse on the receiving end experiences significant hurt and an emotional letdown.

This gentleman sought our help to secure employment after an extended layoff of eleven months. His wife of 27 years accompanied him to the initial session. He complained that his wife gave little support to his efforts to find employment, which lately added to the depression he had experienced since the layoff, and he was now on an antidepressant. He added that he was spending a good amount of time at his home computer and hoped he might find work he could do at home, perhaps even create an online business. This just seemed to anger his wife even more.

An additional stressor was that his wife had resumed working after years of being at home. Her perception was that for several months her husband had spent many hours "just sitting around the house." She felt put upon and unappreciated to suddenly find herself the family breadwinner and resented what appeared to be her husband's idleness. As a result, she had grown emotionally distant from him.

Although she admitted that his behavior was uncharacteristic, she could not seem to control her anger and described most of her conversations with him as being, "My words are like daggers from my mouth to his ears." She realized she needed to be kinder, but his slovenly appearance and the recent addition of an antidepressant only produced more anger in her rather than compassion.

Approximately five months into the layoff, the couple agreed that their marriage was being tested and for a time had seen a pastoral counselor. As Christians they believed in God's power to bring forth a new job and to restore their marriage, and they both deeply regretted the arguments that had erupted.

During a brief period when things had improved, they had stopped seeing the counselor. Unfortunately, the wife's criticisms resumed several weeks later when the husband still had not found employment. At the end of our initial visit, the couple was referred for marriage counseling due to the personal stress each partner identified at that visit.

Over the next four months, we assisted this gentleman in updating his resume and refining his job interview skills for today's job market. Ultimately, he was successful in securing a job in his previous line of work with a rival company and received a raise based on the leadership qualities he demonstrated on interview.

When we saw him three weeks thereafter, he reported

that the couple was progressing well in marriage counseling, that he had stopped his antidepressant, and that his wife was continuing in her job. Being hired with a raise had certainly helped the couple's marital stress, he said, but they had always had faith that God would provide a way despite the turmoil they experienced. Over the years they had learned to forgive each other, and this "test" had strengthened them individually and as a couple.

Exercise #20

Questions for Small Group Discussion and / or Personal Reflection

1.   To what extent would you say you are a true partner in the work of your spouse, whether it is at home or in the marketplace?

2.   What would it look like if one spouse in a marriage harbored anger or resentment toward the other for a lack of vocational support? Use descriptive words and actions to report your view.

3.   Have you seen marriages that struggle with the aforementioned issues? If so and without identifying the people involved, share your observations of what is occurring.

Activity

Observe your interaction and communication with your spouse over the course of the next week. See if you can identify areas in which you may be too critical. Try finding at least one thing (genuine and legitimate) that you notice each day that is a positive characteristic or action on the part of your spouse. Find creative ways to share your observations without seeming too formulaic. If this is an area for some big improvements, a sudden change may cause too much suspicion and feelings of being manipulated. In these situations, see if you can catch your spouse in the act of doing or being something noteworthy, and mention it once in a while.

Countless wives have given their husbands the ultimatum, "Either you find a job by X day or I'm leaving." (How's that for 'til death do us part?)

"You need to persevere so that when you have done the will of God, you will receive what He has promised."
Hebrews 10:36

When neither spouse works, the stress that exists between them can disrupt the couple to the point that the marriage potentially ends in divorce. Some degree of depression is to be expected with job loss and will be experienced on some level. When men hear an ultimatum from their wives, the effect can be devastating to their self-esteem and push them even further into depression. Not only is the husband faced with very complicated feelings of failure from the loss of a job, but the resulting strife that develops between the couple may become irreparable.

In this case, the husband had been regularly employed for nine years and without a job four months at the time he came to us. He had pursued employment with weekly job interviews but with disappointing results and sought our help to target potential new markets. His wife had quit her job four months into a difficult pregnancy that unfortunately coincided with our client's loss of work, and the savings they had accumulated had diminished significantly.

Our client confessed that the couple's faith was being tested in ways he never could have imagined, that they were trying as hard as possible to be patient and tolerant with each other and their circumstances, but that their patience and faith were stretched far beyond normal limits.

Already suffering great emotional anguish, our client felt further pushed over the edge after his wife repeatedly threatened to leave if he did not find a job. He expressed understanding of her frustration and believed the pressure she felt was a result of difficulties with the pregnancy compounded by his being out of work. But after hearing her threats over the course of several weeks, he felt like leaving home himself and had openly expressed such thoughts to his wife. This was devastating to them both because, before their current problems, they had been devoted to each other and greatly anticipated the birth of their first child. They saw themselves as devout believers, but after months of both being unemployed and the wife's pregnancy complications, they were very concerned they would not be able to carry their burden to a successful outcome.

With career, church and family support, the couple's faith in God's Word and in each other prevailed as they persevered. One month before his wife's delivery of a healthy baby, our client secured a job that met their financial needs. As his wife regained her physical strength, the couple continued to repair their marriage.

Exercise #21

Questions for Small Group Discussion and / or Personal Reflection

1.   What would you do to comfort someone experiencing anguish amidst a job loss?

2.   When was the last time your faith was really tested? How did you handle it? Would you change anything about your response the next time?

Activities

Find someone experiencing a fair amount of turmoil at work. Ask them if there is anything you can do to help. Try something fun like a movie and then go somewhere afterward. Invite your friend to share thoughts and feelings about circumstances at work. Listen and affirm them without trying to solve their problems.

How might you adjust your attitude on the way home the next time you are having a really bad day at work or facing the perils of unemployment?

A type "A" businesswoman wants to move up the corporate ladder in spite of her deepest longing to remain in her current house and grow her most important relationships. She feels she needs $150,000.

"Do not love the world or anything in the world. If anyone loves the world, the love of the Father is not in him. For everything in the world—the cravings of sinful man, the lust of his eyes and the boasting of what he has and does—comes not from the Father but from the world. The world and its desires pass away, but the man who does the will of God lives forever."
1 John 2:15-17

Tremendous drive characterizes type "A" individuals. They are frequently the first born child in a family, often take a leadership role with their siblings, and generally demonstrate a capacity for responsibility in many of their endeavors. These characteristics may also exist in families with one child, particularly when one or both parents is a high achiever or expects much from their child.

In our example, the circumstances certainly suggest that this woman is driven to excel at her job and seemingly equates her worth with a significant dollar figure. She appears to measure her worth based on external factors rather than on the essence of who she is as a total person. On the surface, it appears that she equates her value with worldliness.

Our client presented with outstanding job qualifications

seeking a higher paying job in her field on a national level. She had tried through regular local channels and used the standard chain-of-command resources available to her but without satisfaction. We were able to find an opportunity that offered a salary close to what she felt she needed and she was offered the job, which involved a move. However, she experienced significant ambivalence about leaving her home and family.

The degree to which she seemed to associate her self-worth with her salary was apparent, and due to her ambivalence, she agreed to further discussions about this when we brought it to her attention.

We discovered that her drive stemmed from a medical condition in one of the family members that put extreme financial burden on the family. With her talents and business achievements, she saw herself as the most natural member to help alleviate the financial burden and aggressively determined to maximize her abilities to stabilize the situation, at least from a financial standpoint.

This lady had confessed to us that she earnestly sought God's will for her in this situation, but that she felt extremely torn to proceed with what looked for a while like the only alternative: to accept the job and the move.

A strong desire to remain with her family and her determination to help them resulted in her convincing the new company to hire her on a contract basis for a year with full benefits, after which they would consider extending the contract under the same conditions. She was subsequently able to operate a business from home and to remain with her family.

At our last meeting, she affirmed that her faith had indeed sustained her, and she was excited about the new possibilities opening up for her. She felt her priorities were where they should be and that she had honored her commitment to her family and to God.

"Therefore, my dear brothers, stand firm. Let nothing move you. Always give yourselves fully to the work of the Lord, because you know that your labor in the Lord is not in vain." 1 Corinthians 15:58

Exercise #22

Questions for Small Group Discussion and / or Personal Reflection

What are your aspirations for career advancement?

Without making any hasty judgments about whether or not your desires stem from selfish ambition or a yearning to fully utilize your God-given talents, what kind of promotion or position of career advancement would be appealing to you?

Now, let's look at some possible underlying motivations. In what circumstances might you want to climb the proverbial corporate ladder? Be ready to cite your level of understanding as to why you answered as you did.

Activity

Pray about what God's vision might be for your career future. Whether or not you feel like you have "heard from the Lord," establish and write out two or three goals addressing your work life. Reread the scripture passage at the end of this section, **1 Corinthians 15:58.**

A businesswoman was lied to upon hiring at a local bank. Rather than speak poorly about management, she takes the high road and walks with integrity.

"I call on the LORD in my distress, and He answers me. Save me, O LORD, from lying lips and from deceitful tongues. What will He do to you, and what more besides, O deceitful tongue? He will punish you with a warrior's sharp arrows, with burning coals of the broom tree." Psalm 120:1-4

I t's unfortunate when people feel they must lie to each other, as this example represents. On initial contact with this client, she explained that on a recent job interview she had been quoted a certain salary and assured a particular day off she required to maintain volunteer duties at a local charity. Management had guaranteed her there would be no problem with continuing those duties and cited a few examples of other employees with similar responsibilities. She said that, in fact, they actually boasted about their monetary contributions to charity, which she found distasteful and inappropriate.

A few days after being on the job, management informed her that she would not be allowed the time off. When she inquired as to the change in their agreement with her, she was told that after checking with their district manager, it was felt that the company had already "bent the rules" for too many employees and could not honor their word in this matter.

Due to her strong volunteer commitments, and rather than

fight a battle she felt she would not win, she quietly resigned her new position after two weeks. This lady chose to follow God's teachings and forgave those who lied to her.

> "He who is kind to the poor lends to the LORD, and He will reward him for what he has done." Proverbs 19:17

Our role in helping this woman was to provide information about job opportunities in surrounding areas that might allow the latitude she needed for her volunteer work. When from unknown sources a bank competitor heard how she had been unfairly dealt with, they offered her a job before we could assist her further.

The ethical and moral character this lady demonstrated undoubtedly helped her to secure a position by an employer who appreciated her values.

Exercise #23

Questions for Small Group Discussion and / or Personal Reflection

1. Where do you see a lack of integrity or poor ethics in your experience in the marketplace? Please write down specific examples.

2. Have you been wronged or treated in such a way as to conclude that there was a real lack of integrity in this situation? Describe the situation.

3. How would you handle a similar situation of "taking the high road" and standing up for integrity?

4. What do you think people would say when asked about the quality of integrity in your life? Are there any areas that come to mind where you believe some enhancements are needed?

Application

The next time you are treated poorly by a service provider of some sort, make it a point to bring it to their attention. You may want to share expectations of how the situation could be handled with higher integrity.

Take a personal inventory of your integrity level. Use a 1 to 5 scale with 5 representing excellent, 3 average, and 1 poor. Are you happy with your scores?

Quality	Rating
Honesty	_____
Trustworthiness	_____
Dependability	_____
Ethical	_____
Other-centered	_____
Obey authority	_____

A successful entrepreneur (around 50 years old) decides to sell his business so he can have more time for ministry and community development interests. He now leads a tremendous outreach to the inner city.

May the LORD repay you for what you have done. May you be richly rewarded by the LORD, the God of Israel, under whose wings you have come to take refuge." Ruth 2:12

This client came to us seeking to assist his employees in securing other employment as a result of the sale of his business. After years as a profitable businessperson, he now sought to fulfill the call of God in his life in a more pronounced way.

Feeling he had been blessed with many years of success, he wanted to make the transition for his employees as smooth as possible, and we were glad to provide our services to them all.

Our client initially approached us bringing letters of recommendation and a synopsis of each employee's duties and capabilities. We found this to be an extraordinary gesture on his part, one we had never encountered to this degree. The company's reputation for quality service, combined with the recommendations for each employee, made other placements a fairly simple matter.

To the best of our knowledge, all of the former employees have been successfully hired in new positions. Many of them have volunteered their time and talents to continue working with him, whom they described as a generous man who went above and beyond what was expected on their behalf, a trait many felt contributed greatly to his successful career. He had always had a kind word for others and shown a willingness to help people.

> "From the fruit of his lips a man is filled with good things as surely as the work of his hands rewards him."
> Proverbs 12:14

Exercise #24

Questions for Small Group Discussion and / or Personal Reflection

1. How could a professional with an average income and lifestyle contribute to ministry and / or community development interests?

2. In your situation, given your likely time demands, is it realistic for you to increase your involvement in charitable causes? Or do you feel pretty good about your present level of outreach to others?

3. What needs do you see in your church, area non-profits and community service organizations, and in your city at large? What would you want to address if money wasn't an object? Just have fun with this question and let yourself dream a little. You never know...God may be planting a seed in your heart to act on your vision at some point in time.

Activities

1. Evaluate your current level of involvement in charitable or service opportunities. There is a season

for everything, so don't feel like you have to charge into your local church, for instance, and start changing diapers.

2.   Prayerfully seek God's counsel in this area of life. Does He have a mission for you to participate in? What might be one goal for this area of your life—even if it is to pick up a pamphlet and investigate a cause you have been curious about?

Many clients sit at home and wait for the phone to ring. They are too afraid to call someone they don't know and lack faith that God is moving in and through their process.

"I love you, O LORD, my strength. The LORD is my rock, my fortress and my deliverer; my God is my rock, in whom I take refuge. He is my shield and the horn of my salvation, my stronghold." Psalm 18:1-2

It is desirable, and at times imperative, that people seeking jobs demonstrate certain characteristics: determination, self-motivation, energy, sincerity, honesty, ingenuity, perseverance, and an interest in their new employer. Employers typically seek applicants with the required job skills who display initiative and desirable assets favorable to the company. Applicants who are timid generally experience a more difficult time securing a job, often due to shyness and being uncomfortable in an interview situation. When we encounter such clients, we try to help them find inner strength to be more animated and assertive and, thereby, display more self-confidence.

A shy young man was scheduled for a job interview in three weeks and, with the strong support of a friend, found the courage to contact us. We contracted to build up his weak interview skills, which once strengthened would enhance his chances of being hired for a position he was qualified for and which he wanted. He claimed to be a man of faith but felt that his prayer life was suffering due to his fears, and that his connection to God was temporarily blocked. Our agreement to help him "fine-tune" his interview skills provided the impetus to help him over this hurdle.

We focused on strengths he definitely possessed and encouraged him to concentrate on the positive energy within and all around him. The degree of support from others was truly admirable in this young man's situation, particularly the support he received from his church group, which continued to pray with him for strength to overcome his fears. As his confidence improved, his motivation to be awarded the job proved the final key to actually being hired. When we last heard from him six months later, he had earned a bonus for exceptional job performance and anticipated a substantial raise at his annual review.

People need not feel fear when they pray and seek God and know that He is working on their behalf, as in this young man's situation. Those who are reluctant or passive can find strength and protection in God's Word. If you find yourself gripped by fear and surrounded by negative forces, learn to concentrate on the positive energy all around you. Call upon the name of the Lord to sustain you in times of fear, weakness and trouble.

Exercise #25

Questions for Small Group Discussion and / or Personal
Reflection

1. Have you ever experienced call reluctance or fear of
    talking with someone you don't know? Where does
    this seem to surface the most in your life?

2. Public speaking is rated as the #1 fear in America (even
    over death). Why do you think people experience so
    much anxiety addressing a group?

Activities

At your next social outing, make it a point to introduce
yourself and start a conversation with a new person. You'll
find that whether you need to become more social or make
networking calls in a job search that practice and trust in the
Lord makes all the difference in the world. When might you be
able to do this?

Our scripture verse for this section, **Psalm 18:1-2**, says that
the Lord is our strength, a rock, fortress and deliverer. He is our

source of refuge, a shield and a stronghold. Engage in prayer with regards to this issue. Confess areas where you have been more concerned with the approval of people rather than pleasing the Lord. Offer praise for the qualities that characterize His reliability and trustworthiness. Ask Him to help you put your complete confidence in His loving protection and strength to face those things you are afraid of.

A young college graduate from Africa refuses to join with his peers. His fellow countrymen went ahead and got jobs in the U.S. without the proper paperwork, which is illegal. The young graduate waited until he was legal and is now suffering the temporary consequences of a tight job market.

"Even my close friend, whom I trusted, he who shared my bread, has lifted up his heel against me. But you, O LORD, have mercy on me; raise me up, that I may repay them. I know that you are pleased with me, for my enemy does not triumph over me. In my integrity you uphold me and set me in your presence forever." Psalm 41:9-12

When this young man came to us, he was feeling frustrated, dejected and betrayed, but as he told us the entire story of why he sought our services, it was apparent that he was a young man of integrity and honor. Initially he felt alone and unsupported because he had taken a stand against his friends, whose actions were less honorable or legal than his. He openly proclaimed his belief that God would lead him through this difficult time, but was concerned that he would not be able to survive a lengthy financial wait for a job.

"Stand firm then, with the belt of truth buckled around your waist, with the breastplate of righteousness in place, and with your feet fitted with the readiness that comes from the gospel of peace. In addition to all this, take up the shield of faith, with which you can extinguish all the flaming arrows of the evil one." Ephesians 6:14-16

We began seeing him on a regular basis to provide weekly job leads and to lessen the sense of betrayal he felt from his friends and the guilt he experienced in taking a stand against them. He occasionally worked on an irregular or short-term basis while seeking our assistance in improving his employment potential, and he gained additional support by joining an area church where members prayed for his guidance.

With periodic career counseling sessions and his support network, this young graduate developed the confidence he needed to sustain through troubled times as he continued searching for a job in his preferred field. He made many positive contacts both through and outside our office. To date, he is still interviewing for his ideal job, and we feel it is only a matter of time before this young man will find the employment he wants.

Exercise #26

Questions for Small Group Discussion and / or Personal Reflection

1. Have you ever taken a stand for the ethical route in decision-making? Were you alone in your commitment to high morale standards? Share your experience.

2. Ephesians 6:16 explains that we are to "take up the shield of faith, with which you can extinguish all the flaming arrows of the evil one." What do you think the scripture might be describing when it talks about a "shield of faith"?

3. In the aforementioned passage, it talks about protection from the "flaming arrows of the evil one." What are some of your opinions about the possible meaning of this portion of the Bible?

Activities

1. Identify a "flaming arrow" the evil one seems to be targeting at you. Pray that God would allow you to be victorious in this battle, whether it is more pronounced at work or at home, employed or in transition.

2. The next time you catch yourself in a downward spiral, reflect on the promise that God has equipped us with

the armor we need to win any battle we face. Fight deception, negative thinking, persecution, lies from the evil one in attempts to get you to quit, and any other obstacles to the abundant Christian life. The battle is won by faith—belief without evidence. Trust in an unseen God. If He had the power to create the universe, He is certainly sufficient to meet our needs.

CONCLUSION

"Teach me thy way, O LORD; I will walk in thy truth:
unite my heart to fear thy name." Psalm 86:11

We began by seeking a roadmap to sanity for life. Why do we need a roadmap? Because our society offers many distractions that can easily divert our attention away from what is truly important in life, frequently affecting work and home balance. While numerous guidelines and strategies are available in the general marketplace for "better living," our approach is aimed at reaching deeper levels of personal fulfillment and satisfaction.

We believe that there is only "one boss" and that is God, our Lord Jesus Christ, and that wisdom and direction for successful living come from the Word of God, His Holy Bible.

Through career coaching services, we assist people having difficult work-related issues with how to survive in the workplace using faith-based principles as foundations for a better life. We help them find jobs and problem-solve in order to attain a healthy balance of professional, personal and home life, as well as the authentic success they seek.

We are concerned with our clients' quality of life because we know that God has the very best plans for them, despite any problems they may temporarily experience. Our goal is to help our clients uncover wonderful opportunities that God presents through the disguise of problems, heartaches, disappointments and, at times, tragedies.

The theme of our book has targeted problems Christians face in the workplace and offered solutions based on biblical principles. The situations discussed are also representative of problems faced by non-Christians, and we trust that God will bring forth those readers whom He calls to these pages, which have been inspired by Him.

We hope, Dear Reader, that we have helped you "take out the trash" that clogs your mind, understanding that solutions exist for all problems and that Jesus will guide you through them and put people in your life to help in this process.

We hope that your vision is now open to new possibilities and that you have experienced a mindset adjustment that helps to clear the cobwebs of your thinking and perceptions about your life in general.

We encourage you to continue your walk with God, to reach out to others, and to allow others to reach inside and touch your life.

You matter to us, and we are available to help you with career issues and to point you to a direction where your life reflects God's presence.

We thank you sincerely for your interaction with us.

Order Multiple Copies of "Winning"

Winning At Work While Balancing Your Life: Career Coaching For Authentic Success is also available in bulk quantities at discounted prices for your special group needs. For additional information contact either Scott or Cynthia at:

http://www.winning-atwork.com

Or you can reach them at the following locations:

(Scott) Scott@CareerImpact.org (501-231-2532)
http://www.careerimpact.org

(Cynthia) info@cynrje.com (757-331-2218)
http://www.cynrje.com

Additional single copies of **Winning** are also available from the above locations.

And be sure to sign up for your FREE "Winning At Work Newsletter" when you visit:

http://www.winning-atwork.com
or
http://www.careerimpact.org

Special Author Opportunities

D r. Scott Rosenthal, President of Career Impact and Co-Director of CrossRoads Group, offers career and life coaching to enhance your personal and professional life. He is a doctoral level, state licensed counselor and an ordained minister who has helped hundreds of people accomplish amazing goals, make changes of a lifetime and realize their dreams. Get Scott's FREE 20-minute consultation with no obligation. Take advantage of his special offer by sending an email to Scott@CareerImpact.org.

Get a FREE COPY of Scott's downloadable ebook **Believers, Be Armed!** with your purchase of **Winning** by visiting http://www.winning-atwork.com.

Cynthia Peavler Bull, founder of CYN-R-JE Consultants, LLC™, has helped many international authors, marketers and motivational speakers reach new heights and add greater value to their products through her writing and editing services. To get a 50% DISCOUNT on your next writing or editing project contact her at info@cynrje.com.

Cynthia is also a medical transcriptionist and offers career guidance in her book **How To Be A Medical Transcriptionist: A Beginner's Guide To Real Facts And Inside Secrets That Lead To A Successful Career**. For more information visit http://www.transcription-medical.com.

Recommended Products for Spiritual Enlightenment, Career Guidance, and Character Development

Order these books from **Scott@CareerImpact.org**

Believers, Be Armed! by Dr. Scott Rosenthal ($9.95): Free with **Winning!** This companion Ebook to **Winning** tells more about how people can achieve authentic success, true significance, and balance in work and life. Be sure to get your FREE COPY.

Maximizing Your Leadership Potential — From God's Perspective, by Dr. Scott Rosenthal ($19.95): This Ebook gives you a fresh sense of purpose for your work that will provide lasting meaning and motivation. Gain a greater sense of self- respect and ability to witness for Jesus Christ in the workplace and enjoy a closer relationship with Him throughout the workweek. Plus, learn principles of financial prosperity and how to decrease debt.

The Unsung Heroes of Faith, by Career Impact ($7.95): Looking for Spiritual Inspiration? There are many inspiring and well-known Bible characters of faith we hear and read about in the scriptures. This Ebook draws your attention to some Bible characters you have perhaps heard little of before. Hopefully, these unsung heroes of faith will inspire you to grow to greater heights in your walk with the Lord.

How Do You See? by Career Impact ($4.95): You've heard it said, "Seeing is believing." But is everything you see really all there is to be seen? With God, there is more "to see" than what we just see with our eyes. Put on your "Spiritual Glasses" and read this Ebook to find new insights on situations you face every day, how to see through the haze that clouds your vision and beyond trials to opportunities that may lie within. Learn how to recognize God's handiwork in today's world and focus on His plan.

The Will of God, by Career Impact ($4.95): Does God have a will for every minute detail in your life? Whether you believe God may or may not be involved in every tiny detail or in the choices we make, He does have a "will" for our lives—here on earth and for our heavenly life. Read this Ebook and examine God's Will as stated in the New Testament and learn more about the "Will of God."

Order these books from Cynthia at **info@cynrje.com**

Walking With The Wise Entrepreneur, by Mentors Magazine.com with contributing writer Cynthia Peavler Bull ($16.95): Inspirational mentors and millionaires teach secrets of prosperity in business and life. Read motivational stories of contributors like Donald Trump, Chuck Norris, Suze Orman and John Assaraf as well as 'ordinary' entrepreneurs and learn strategies and guidance from the masters to reach your life goals. (Available in soft cover edition)

You've Been Set Up For a Setback...And It Was An Inside Job, by Joseph N. Tapper ($12.95): Challenges can be exciting if you understand why they come. There is no need to get upset, frustrated or angry. We find that praise will be our answer to trouble whenever it shows up on our doorstep. God has to prepare us to receive our blessings, so when troubles come, we will know why and exactly what to do. A person's height is not measured in inches but by how tall they stand under adversity. A person's true character is revealed when that person is faced with adversity. People know you by how you react to challenges.

Your reaction is the real you, and this is what we can improve upon through self-development. (Available in soft cover edition, edited by Cynthia)

Seeds Of Character, by Joseph N. Tapper ($7.95): A daily handbook to help in the development of character. It's fun and simple, and with daily use you might find the steps easy to do forever. (Available in soft cover edition, edited by Cynthia)

The Acorn and The Peanut, by Joseph N. Tapper ($7.95): A simple little story designed to help you develop your potential to look beyond what you see and find hidden potential in others. No longer will you stop at skin color, culture, physical makeup or race. New friends await you. All you have to do is give them a chance. (Available in soft cover edition, edited by Cynthia)

Notes

Made in the USA